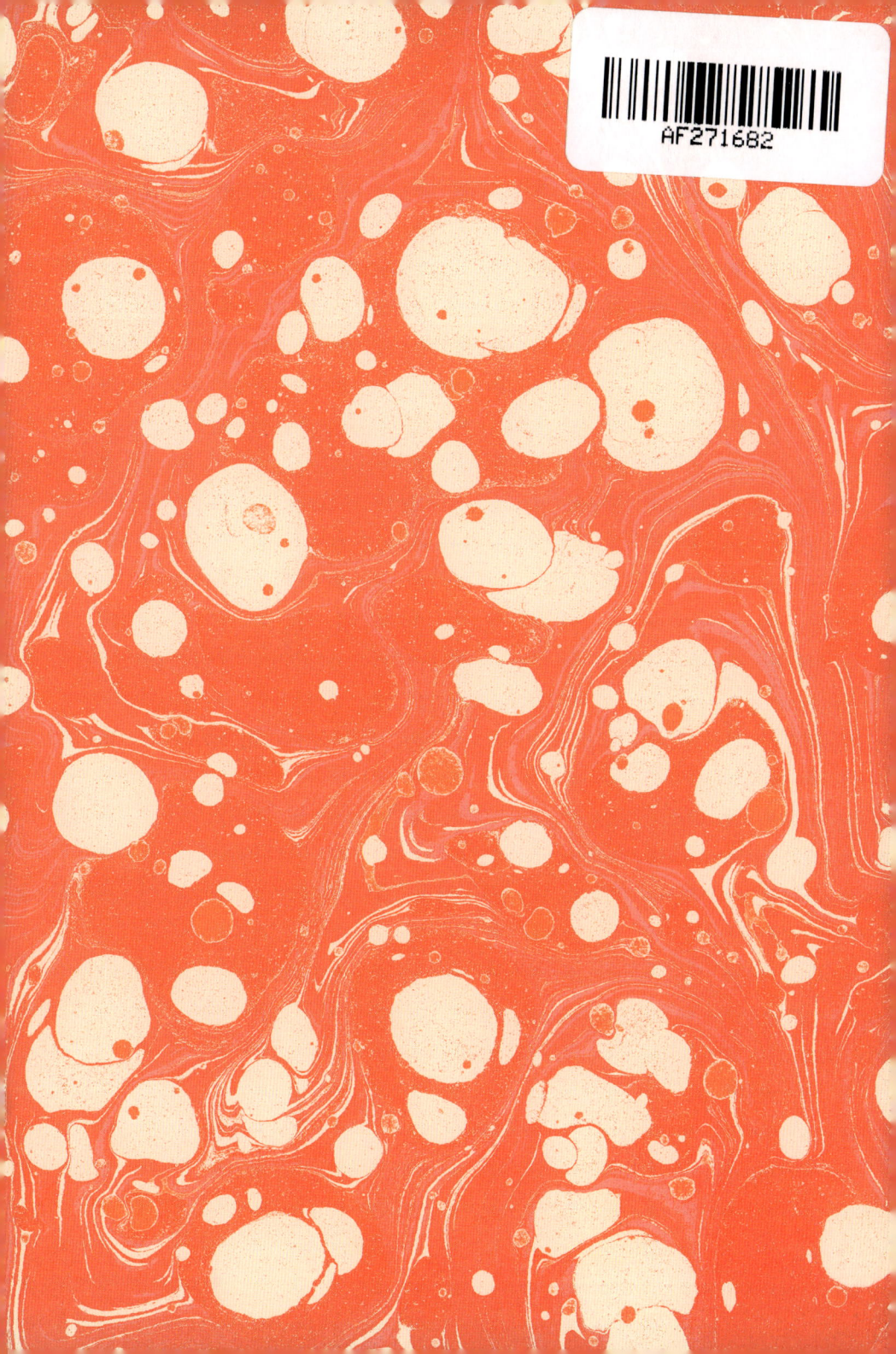

WHAT ART CAN TELL US ABOUT LOVE

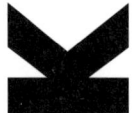

First published in Great Britain in 2025 by Laurence King,
an imprint of The Orion Publishing Group Ltd, Carmelite House,
50 Victoria Embankment, London EC4Y 0DZ

An Hachette UK Company

10 9 8 7 6 5 4 3 2 1

A CIP catalogue record for this book is available
from the British Library.

ISBN (Hardback) 978 1 39962 096 3
ISBN (eBook) 978 1 39962 097 0

Commissioning Editor: Laura Paton
Art Director: Liam Relph
Designer: Dan Jackson
Picture Researcher: Emily Taylor
Senior Production Controller: Sarah Cook

Typeface: Garamond Premier Pro
Text paper: 140gsm Golden Sun Woodfree
Endpapers: 140gsm Golden Sun Woodfree
Case: 5/0 (CMYK + PMS 940U) on 130gsm
Chinese Zhimei Pure woodfree FSC

Front cover: *Self-Portrait as a Tehuana*
(or *Diego on My Mind*), Frida Kahlo, 1943

Origination by F1 Colour
Printed in China by C&C Offset Printing Co. Limited

www.laurenceking.com
www.orionbooks.co.uk

WHAT ART CAN TELL US ABOUT LOVE

NICK TREND

LAURENCE KING

For Sophie, Billy and Eleanor

Contents

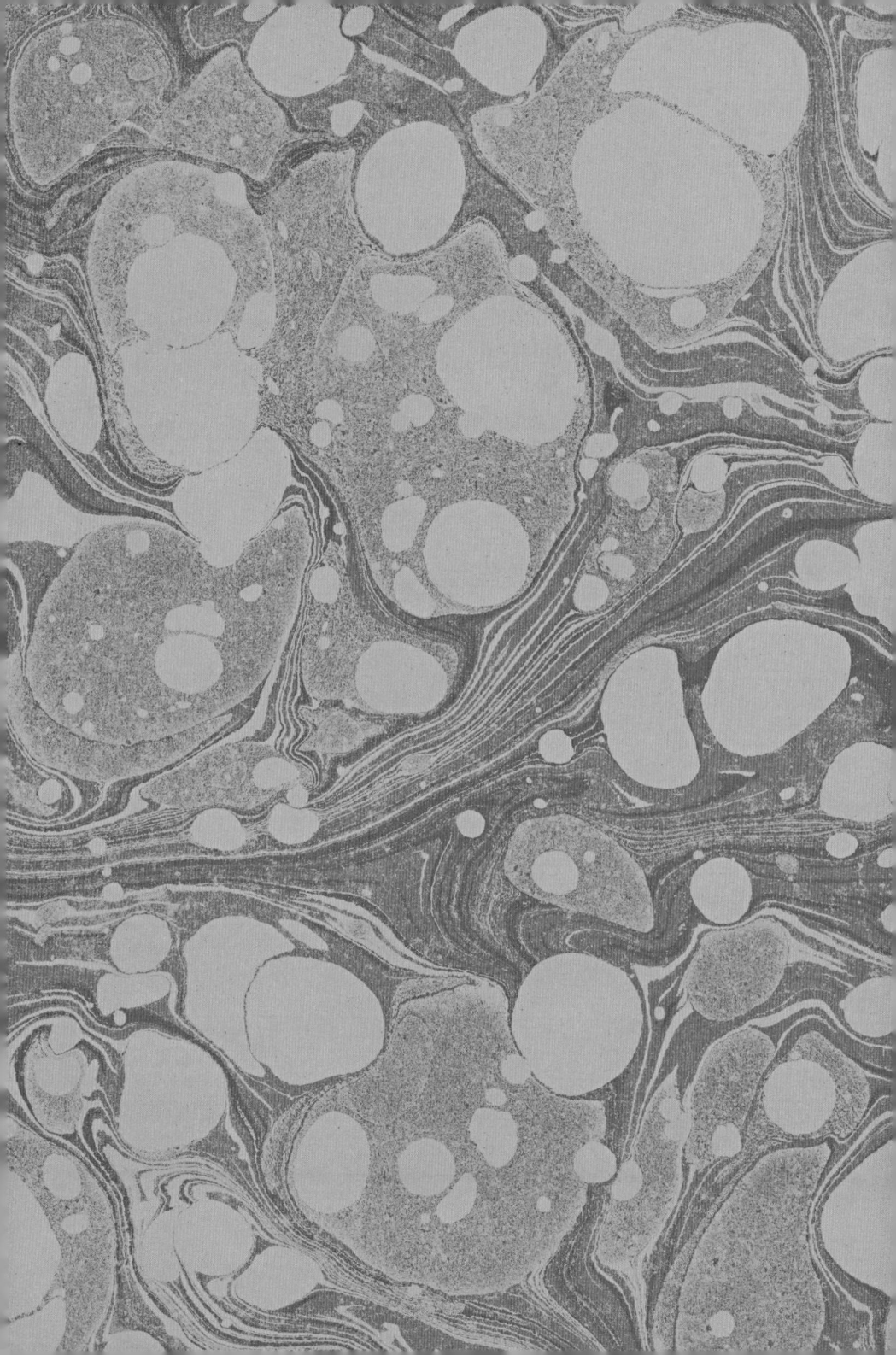

Introduction

How many songs are inspired by love? How many poems, novels, fairy tales and films unfold around a romance? They are what we so often fall back on to try to understand, or simply cope with, that most complicated, most powerful and most all-encompassing of emotions. And there is no doubt that love stories and heartfelt ballads offer consolation, inspiration and insights into our deepest passions. But what about pictures? What can art tell us about love?

It's not something we often consider very directly. We talk about the inspiration of 'muses', but that's an alienating word which aggrandizes artists and suggests that they are somehow different from ordinary people. They aren't. And we don't need to attribute an artist's motivation to some sort of classical ideal. They are affected by emotion, disappointment and the chemistry of desire just like the rest of us. They are just able to express the complications more eloquently.

True, some – like Marc Chagall – seem to idealize their feelings. His floating, dreamlike images are clearly infused with his gentle, exultant adoration of his wife, Bella. But there are many, many different expressions of love in art – sometimes blatant and daring, often subtle or even secret. And to understand them we need to know how to read the imagery, how to recognize the signs and tease out the meanings.

Perhaps sometimes we forget, for example, that every portrait involves two people. The sitter is not alone. Those eyes which today we think are looking at us were, in reality, once focused on the painter standing beside the easel. When it turns out that the two of them were in love with each other, everything suddenly becomes more complicated – and much more interesting. The image we see is not just an attempt at a likeness. It doesn't simply represent a commercial transaction – it is a reflection of the artist's own deepest feelings. And we are right there, in the midst of the affair, caught in the sight-lines between two lovers.

Often we can sense the desire in the clear-cut, voyeuristic experience we draw from erotic art. The meeting between Tamara de Lempicka and a woman called Rafaela, whom she encountered in a park in 1927, resulted in several highly charged nude portraits. They are a powerful evocation of that feeling which so often colours the early stages of love – lust.

But often in the art of love, the clues to its meanings are much more subtle, and we have to look more closely and think more carefully to detect tension or flirtation, desire or bashfulness. We may have to be alert to the tiniest detail or most bizarre twist to give us the insights we seek. Why, in Édouard Manet's portrait of Berthe Morisot, is there so much emphasis on her pink shoe? Why did Sylvia Sleigh depict her husband with a group of naked men in a Turkish bath?

We must remember that love paintings don't have to be portraits. Could Henry Fuseli's depiction of a nightmare stem from frustrated desire? And what, exactly, are we to make of Georgia O'Keeffe's seemingly erotic flower and shell paintings?

Love, as we well know, means different things to different people at different times. It has its ecstasies and its agonies; it can blossom into a deep devotion or burn out and end in tears, recrimination or regret. It can inspire dalliance and delight, but also spark obsession and tragedy. Especially fascinating are the pictures where we seem to be witnessing the very moment when two people fall in love. After all, painting can be an act of extraordinary intimacy. Artist and model may be alone for hours. There is ample time for chemistry to stir, no pressure on conversation. Thoughts, secrets, proposals can emerge at their own pace. That seems to have been how the clandestine – and scandalous – liaison started between the artist Filippo Lippi and his model, a beautiful nun called Lucrezia Buti, in 15th-century Tuscany. And perhaps that is what we see in George Clairin's voluptuous painting of Sarah Bernhardt reclining on a chaise longue in Belle Époque Paris. But a picture might also be a deeply felt tribute to a much more established relationship. Rembrandt's paintings of Hendrickje Stoffels and Rubens' portraits of his second wife, Helena, seem to glow with that sort of heartfelt devotion.

Sometimes feelings can be agonisingly one-way. A whole genre of paintings and portraits has been inspired by unrequited love, as when Winslow Homer tried to process the depth of his feelings for Helena de Kay in the 1870s. She gave him little hope of favour, yet allowed herself to be adored from a distance, the subject of his art – eyes always cast down, remote, unobtainable. Sometimes, too, it gets complicated, really complicated. Love triangles are common in the lives of artists and the tangled affairs of Dora Carrington were among the most complicated of all. She fell in love with a gay man, then a gay woman and was rejected by both. She married a man whom she didn't love and then enjoyed a passionate affair with one of his best friends. And she painted or sketched portraits of them all.

Most of us have experienced emotional complications and feelings of rejection at some point in our life. But whether we are in love, been together for decades, are suffering a break up or wrestling with conflicting emotions, art can help us come to terms with the depth and complexity of our feelings. We just need to look carefully and reflect a little. And remember, too, that our own experiences can also help us understand some of history's greatest paintings and the lives, passions and predilections of the men and women who made them.

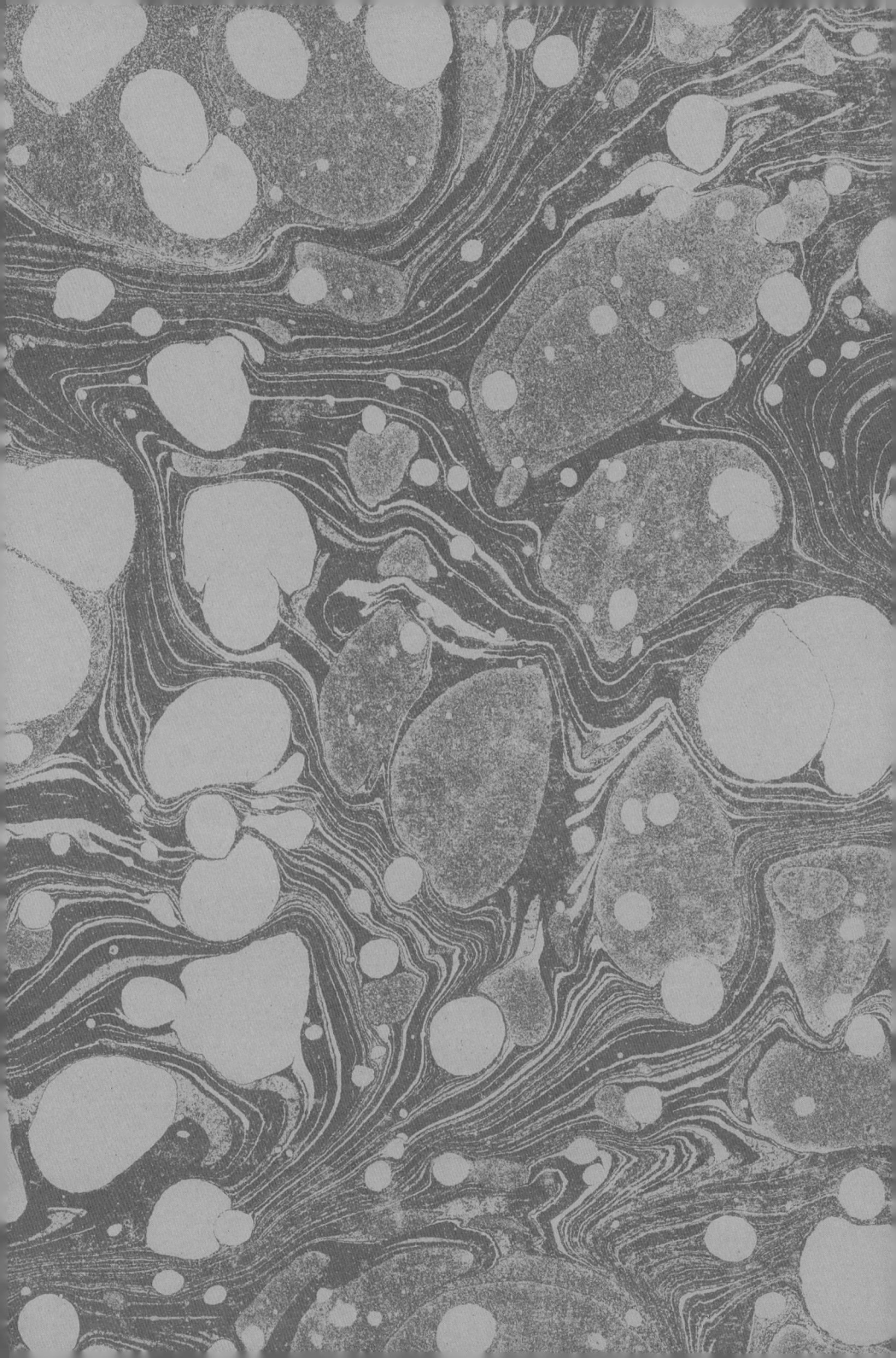

ENDURING

LOVE

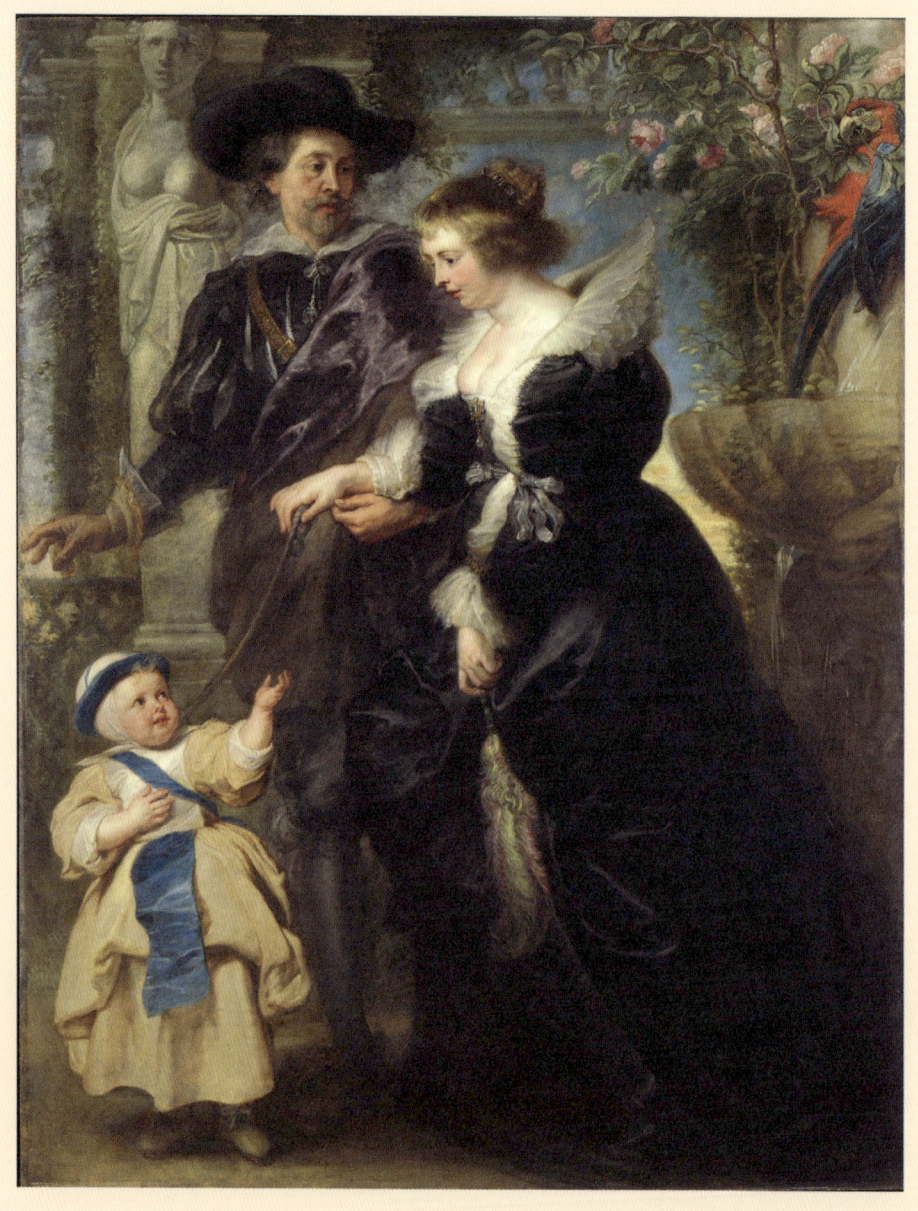

Rubens, Helena Fourment and their Son, Frans, Peter Paul Rubens, c.1635

Total Devotion

Rubens & Helena Fourment

In this family self-portrait, Peter Paul Rubens (1577–1640) depicts himself with his second wife, Helena, and their young son, Frans, strolling in the garden of their house in Antwerp. It is hard to imagine a more tender and devoted tribute from an artist to his wife. Rubens' loving eyes are focused on Helena not just in the painting, but as the artist who is sitting in front of her creating the image. She seems to bathe slightly bashfully in this attention, looking down at Frans, who returns her gaze while simultaneously mirroring his father's gestures and body position. She holds the boy lightly on the end of a leading string and modestly accepts the gentle touch of Rubens' hand on hers as he seems to be showing her the way forward. She is both a cherished wife to Rubens and a loving mother to Frans.

But this painting is not just celebrating the love between the couple and for their son. It is also about projecting Rubens' social status and the perpetuation of his family name. He was now the most sought-after painter in the world. Such were his contacts in the royal courts of Europe that, in 1630, he had brokered a peace treaty between Spain and England and was knighted by both Philip IV and Charles I. The strap across Rubens' chest holds the sheath for his sword, which is indicative of his status as a nobleman. Also, it is Frans, his male heir, whom he includes in the picture, not his eldest child, Clara. And Frans is given a strap-like ribbon across his chest – one day he too will wear a gentleman's sword.

The garden setting is also full of significance. As well as signalling Rubens' status – it had been landscaped in 1610 when he finished building his impressive house in the latest Renaissance style after his return to Antwerp from Rome – it can also be seen as a Garden of Love. Consider the fountain and caryatid statue, whose breasts echo Helena's suggested fertility (note Helena's exposed nipple). The ivy may be a reference to Psalm 128: 'Your wife shall be like a fruitful vine/In the very heart of your house'. And the parrot grasping a rose briar in its beak may also symbolize the pain and pleasure that come with love.

Of course, the image has strong patriarchal overtones that might jar with us today. But it is an extraordinarily tender image and all the evidence suggests that it represents a genuinely heartfelt expression of Rubens' feelings. Helena was the second love of the artist's life. His first wife Isabella had died aged just 34 during a plague outbreak in 1626. He married Helena four years later. The daughter of a wealthy Antwerp silk merchant, she was 16, he was 53, but the age difference doesn't seem to have hampered their happiness. They had five children together, whom Rubens often sketched. He also painted Helena many times. She was the inspiration for some of his famously voluptuous paintings of classical nudes.

By far the most intimate, though, is the *Helena Fourment Het Pelsken* ('Little Fur') portrait, which he made in about 1637. Here Helena is cast, playfully, as Venus, the Goddess of Love. Rubens has posed her both in homage to his great predecessor, Titian, who made several paintings of women in furs, and in imitation of a traditional *Venus Pudica*. Derived from classical sculptures (see p170) this phrase is a reference to the way in which Venus was often depicted trying modestly to cover her nakedness with her hands and arms. Yet, instead of hiding her breasts, Helena here uses her arm to lift them into prominence, nipples

Helena Fourment (Het Pelsken), Peter Paul Rubens, c.1637

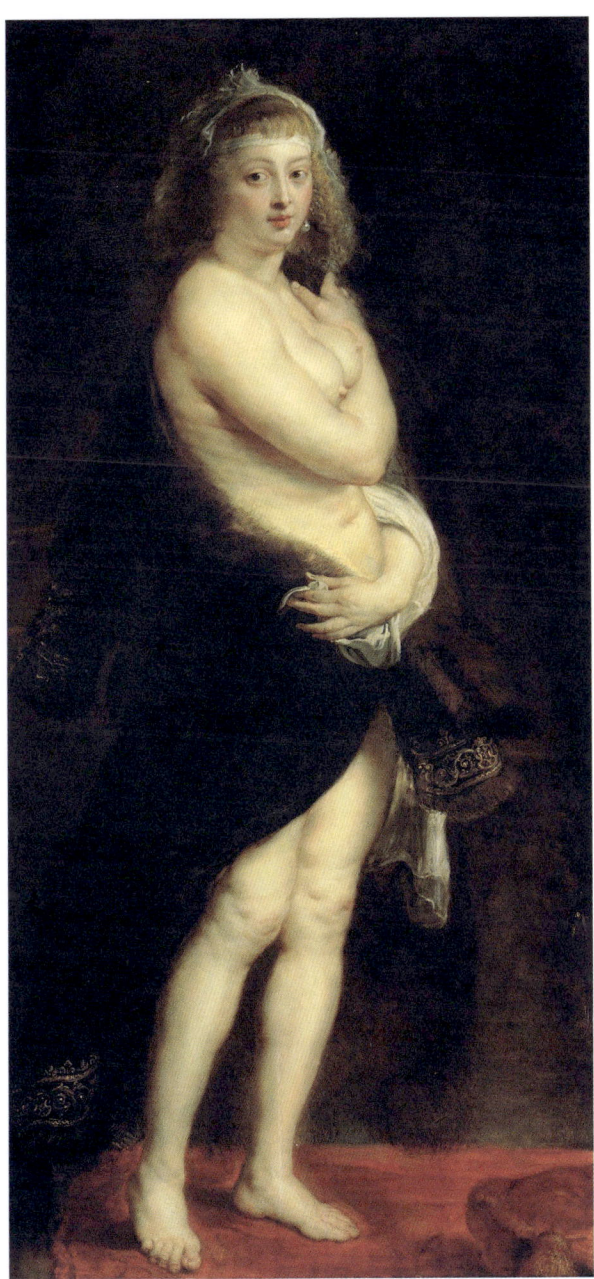

Her body ... with all its slight blemishes, creases and imperfections.

erect. Any modesty we might perhaps perceive in the picture comes from the way she gathers the big fur gown around her body. Here, too, Rubens takes the opportunity to eroticize the gesture. The soft, dark, warm fur not only contrasts with the pale delicacy of her skin, but adds a powerful tactile quality. Seeing fur on flesh like this, we can't help but imagine the sense of warmth it generates and how it must feel to be touching it.

That direct connection with Helena's sensual world is heightened by Rubens' decision to depict her body, not as an idealized form as Titian would have done, with perfectly smooth skin and flowing lines, but with all its slight blemishes, creases and imperfections. It is an intensely private painting which Rubens specifically left to his wife in his will, stipulating that it must not be sold to pay for death duties. After he died in 1640, she kept it until her own death in 1673. She did marry again, but in her will she was careful to leave *Helena Fourment* (*Het Pelsken*) not to her second husband, who outlived her and with whom she had six more children, but instead to the children she had had with Rubens.[1] As they had together decided just before his own death, she was buried alongside Peter Paul in the Rubens Chapel in the church of St James, Antwerp.

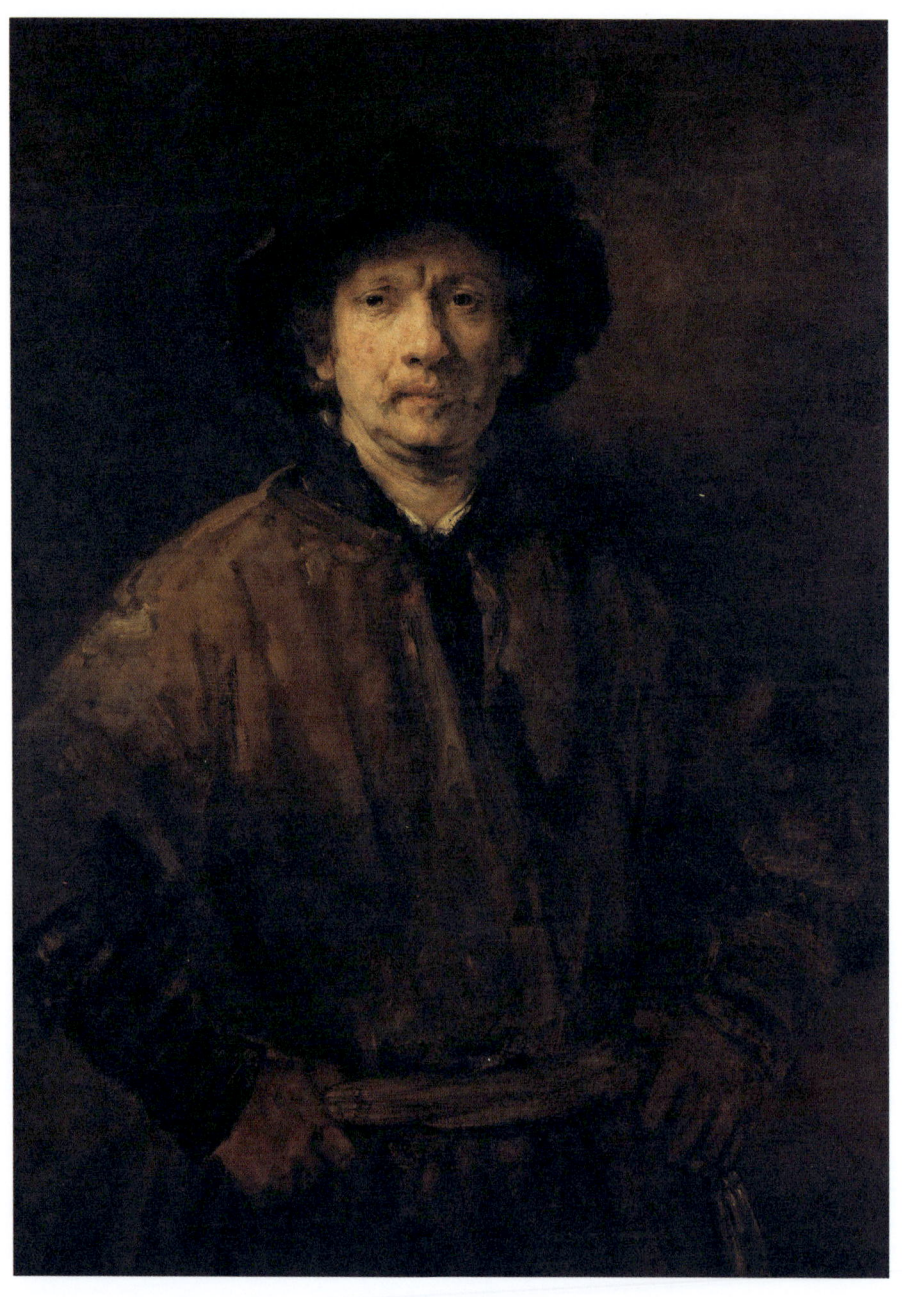

Self-Portrait (or *The Large Self-Portrait*), Rembrandt, 1652

Passion &
Determination

Rembrandt & Hendrickje Stoffels

E motionally, it must have been an extraordinary moment
when Rembrandt made this self-portrait in 1652. Even
though he had painted himself many times in his youth,
he had not done so since his first wife, Saskia, had died 10 years
earlier. He had endured more than a decade of trauma. His
artistic career had stalled; he was running short of money; and
he was beset by legal problems. But now, finally, he set up his
easel, turned to the mirror and raised the courage to look
himself in the eye.

What do we make of the result? Comparing this with his
earlier self-portraits, Rembrandt – now 45 or 46 years old – has
visibly aged. Stress and grief have taken their toll. There are new
shadows under his eyes, the furrow in his brow has deepened
and his chin is heavier.

But his bearing is confident: he stands, arms akimbo,
looking slightly down at us. He is dressed in his artist's smock –
as though he is keen to get on with his work again. And, looking
closely at his face, we can detect a gleam in his eye, emphasized
by the dramatic lighting that rakes in from the left side of the
picture. It is as though, with this portrait, he was declaring that
there was a new purpose in his life. And there was. Rembrandt
had fallen in love.

About three or four years before he made the self-portrait, he had become involved with his maid, Hendrickje Stoffels. There are no letters and no witnesses to testify to the intensity of their relationship, but we can discern from a series of paintings and sketches that Rembrandt made during those years, the remarkable tenderness and intimacy that developed between them.

Two paintings stand out. The first is not a formal portrait, but a depiction of Bathsheba, the Old Testament beauty who was seduced by King David after he spied her bathing naked. Rembrandt used his new lover as a model in what turned out to be one of the most enigmatic and revolutionary paintings of the 17th century. There is none of the traditional idealization of a female nude. Rembrandt doesn't gloss over the slight deformation of her left breast or the heaviness of her stomach. He presents us with what he sees. And perhaps for the first time in Western art – after centuries of artists using the Bathsheba story as an excuse to titillate – Rembrandt also makes us consider what she might be thinking. He depicts the moment just after she has read the letter of proposal sent by King David, when she realizes she must choose between defying the approaches of an all-powerful king or betraying her husband. We can sense her melancholy and resignation as she sits contemplating her fate.

So, paradoxically, this most realistic of nudes is as much about Bathsheba's mind as her body. And it is also, surely, about Hendrickje herself. It is easy to be tempted into making assumptions that can never be proved. We know that she gave birth to their daughter, Cornelia, at the end of October that year. Did she and Rembrandt already know she was pregnant when he was painting her? Is there an analogy between Bathsheba's moment of truth and the harsh reality that Hendrickje knew she must face when she had the baby? Rembrandt could not marry his lover because the money that Saskia had left him was the only thing keeping him from bankruptcy, and there was a provision in the will that meant he would lose the inheritance if he remarried.

Bathsheba at Her Bath, Rembrandt, 1654

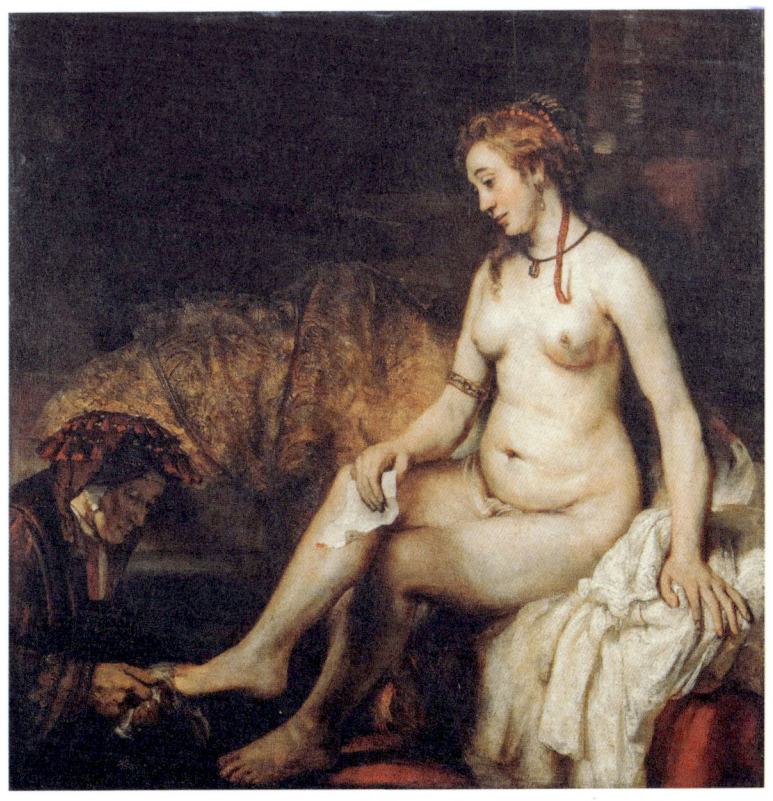

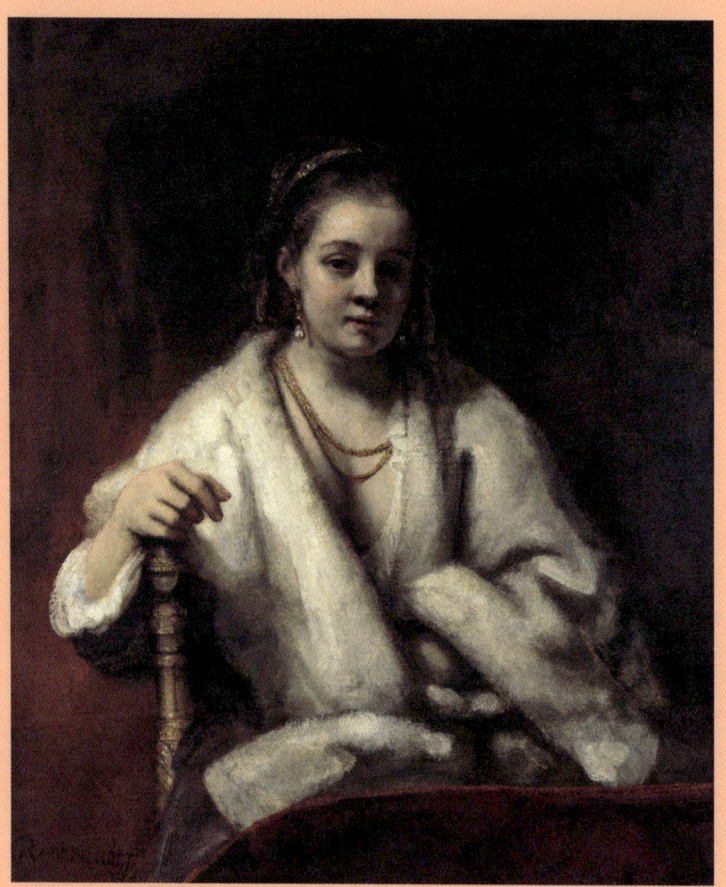

Portrait of Hendrickje Stoffels, Rembrandt, c.1654–1656

So, once it was clear that Hendrickje was pregnant, her happiness must have been tempered by the circumstances. She was to be an unmarried mother – a social and religious pariah. She was publicly shamed and excluded from taking communion.

Things got worse. In 1656 Rembrandt was declared bankrupt and, by 1658, he, Hendrickje, Cornelia and Titus – his son by Saskia – were forced to move to a cheap rented house. Yet Hendrickje seems to have taken responsibility for trying to turn things around. While Rembrandt started to work much harder, she and Titus opened a shop to market his prints and paintings.

Perhaps the portrait of Hendrickje (opposite) captures the most enduring sense of their togetherness and stands as the most fitting memorial to their love. It was made just as Hendrickje was having to get to grips with bankruptcy and life with a young child and yet she radiates a remarkable sense of calmness and poise. She looks directly at us from a slight height, with an almost regal air and a knowing tilt to her head. Her right hand rests on what must be the arm of a chair, yet looks like a sceptre. She wears expensive pearl earrings and a gold chain. There are jewels threaded into ribbons in her hair and a luxurious white fur around her shoulders. Maybe this is the last time she will be able to wear such finery before it has to be sold.

Most revealingly of all, there is a delicious tension between her regal demeanour and the erotic charge of the portrait. Hendrickje's dress of lilac silk is unfastened at the front and her undershirt is partly undone. As she reaches inside her mantle, the shift falls slightly open, revealing the swell of her breasts. Simultaneously, it seems, Rembrandt is expressing not only the depth of his desire but also admiration for his young lover who had sacrificed her respectability to be with him and who was now working so hard to keep the family together.

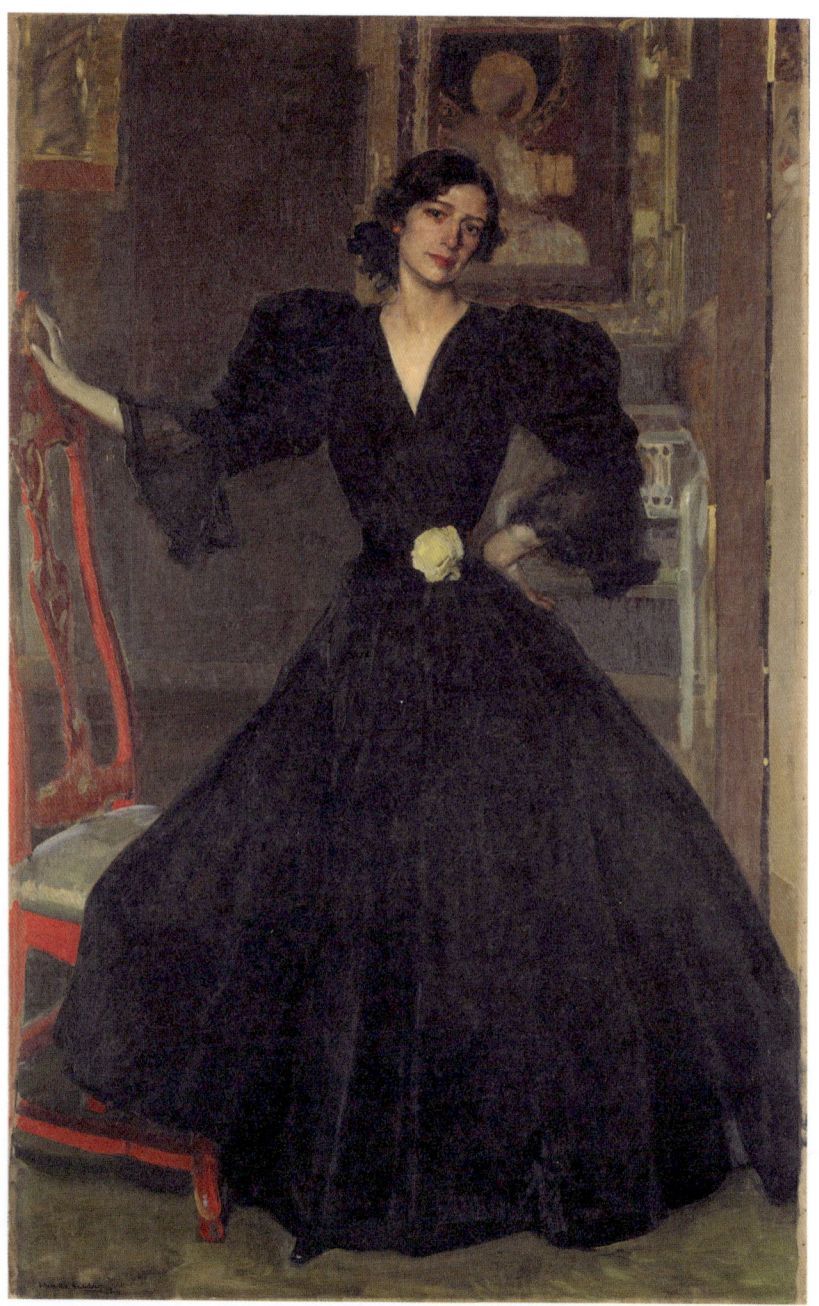

Life-Long Love

Joaquín Sorolla &
Clotilde García del Castillo

In the early years of the 20th century, Joaquín Sorolla (1863–1923) was famous as a 'painter of light', and especially at capturing the effects of the blazing Mediterranean sun. His art was a fresh and vibrant Spanish take on French, but he was also steeped in the great Hispanic tradition of portrait-painting which stretches back to Goya (1746–1828) and Velázquez (1599–1660). It is the 70 portraits that he made of his wife Clotilde over more than 30 years of marriage which give us the greatest insight into the psyche of a man devoted both to his partner and to his art.

Clotilde was the daughter of a photographer who had leant Sorolla studio space at the beginning of his career. They married in 1888 and went on to have three children in a relationship of remarkable intensity and devotion which endured until Sorolla's death in 1923. *Señora de Sorolla in Black*, a life-sized portrait made in 1906 when she was 41 years old, is one of the most fulsome of the many tributes he painted. Clotilde fills the frame with a tremendous sense of presence. Her outstretched arm spans the canvas and yards of black satin seem to cascade from her waist. She has the confident air of a Spanish dancer: hand on her hip, a flower at her girdle, one foot thrust forward, head slightly tilted. Her gaze – as in nearly all the portraits of her – is steady, but is that the faintest of smiles on her lips?

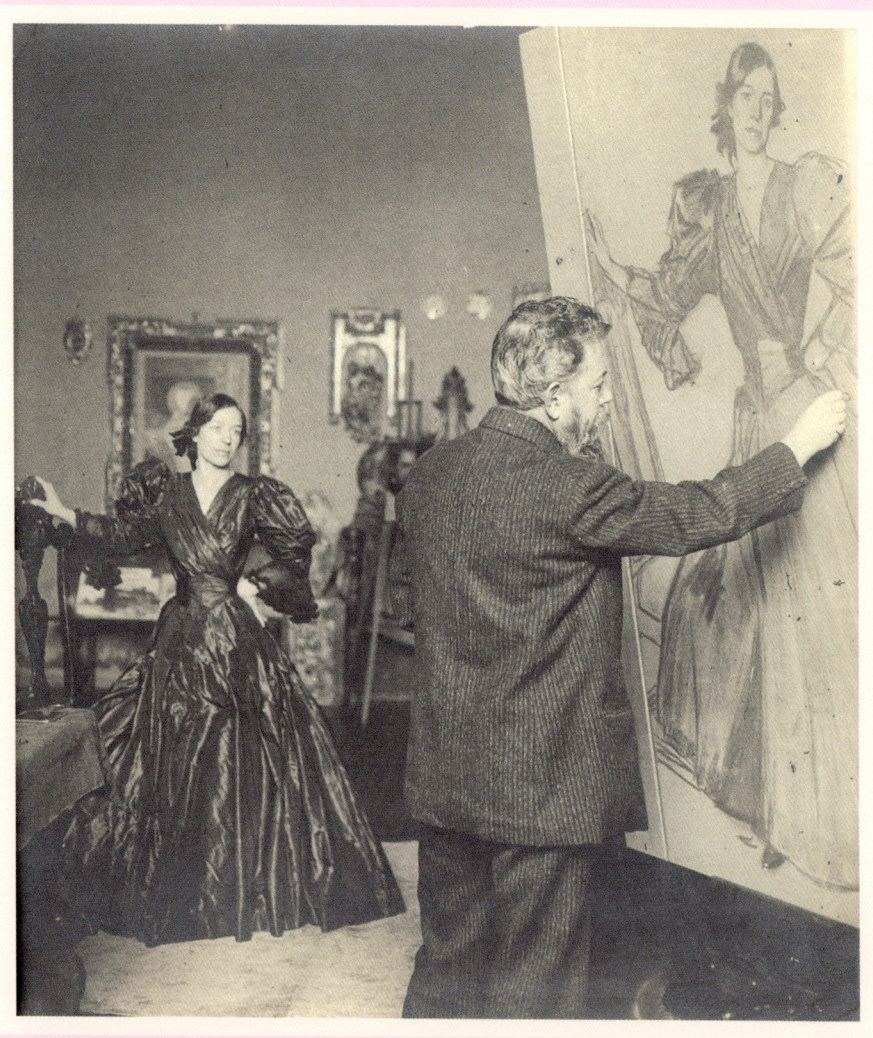

Sorolla painting *Señora de Sorolla in Black*, c.1906

In fact, so glamorous and confident does she look that the portrait could almost be a take from a modern fashion shoot. So waspish is her waist, so stylish her evening gown that it seems as though Sorolla must be exaggerating for effect, presenting us with an idealized impression of the wife he adores. But a photograph taken as Clotilde posed for him confirms how remarkably true to nature the portrait is, not only in its representation of Clotilde, but in the background too. He has positioned her so that the picture of a female saint on the wall appears behind her head in the painting. It was an image which had special significance for both of them. Sorolla made it when they were staying in Assisi shortly after their marriage in 1888 and it is sometimes identified as Saint Clotilde. The close juxtaposition in the portrait could hardly be accidental.

One effect that Sorolla does seem to have moderated is the play of light on the black dress. A high sheen is very noticeable in the photograph, giving a stiffened, more sculptured effect to the folds and creases. But in the painting, Sorolla has softened the fabric, perhaps wanting to present Clotilde herself less stiffly.

Interestingly, the Sorollas did not regard this as a private painting. It was made for an exhibition in Paris in 1906 and then presented at Sorolla's hugely successful exhibition in New York, early in 1909, when it was immediately sold to The Metropolitan Museum of Art. There are echoes of Goya here too, especially of his great portrait of the Duchess of Alba (made in 1797) which had just gone on display in the city.[2] Depicted life-sized, hand on hip in a glamorous black dress, Goya's picture is often seen as a love tribute to the duchess who wears a ring etched with their names and points at the words 'Solo Goya' ('Only Goya') inscribed in the sand at her feet. Sorolla would certainly have known reproductions, and may have seen the painting when it was sold at auction in Paris in 1906.

But it is Clotilde undressed which is the most intimate and adoring of all Sorolla's tributes to his wife and which makes the clearest reference to his artistic heritage. *Female Nude* of

1902, is one of only a handful of nudes which he made during his career. It was painted immediately after he returned from a visit to England to see Velázquez's famous *Rokeby Venus*, then hanging in Rokeby Park in County Durham. In Velázquez's painting, the naked goddess of love lies with her back to us, attended by Cupid who holds up a mirror so we can see the hazy reflection of her face (and she can see us looking at her). Sorolla's response is to lie his goddess in a mirrored pose (that is, head and feet reversed), but without the mirror itself and without Cupid. He repeats Velázquez's palette of pinks and greys, but he intensifies the pinks and – as he did with the black dress – makes the fabrics more sensual. He also crops out nearly all the backdrop at the top of the picture – nothing else matters except the naked woman lying on a luxurious bed stretching out in front of us.

And while Sorolla never formally identified the model, there is no doubt whatsoever that it was Clotilde. Not only are her hair and the shape of her waist giveaways, but instead of staring into a mirror as Velázquez's Venus does, Sorolla depicts her looking intently at the wedding ring on her right hand (the traditional side in Spain) – surely a reference to their own marriage. She is his faithful goddess of love, but shorn of the vanity and fickleness of Venus.

Female Nude, Joaquín Sorolla, 1902

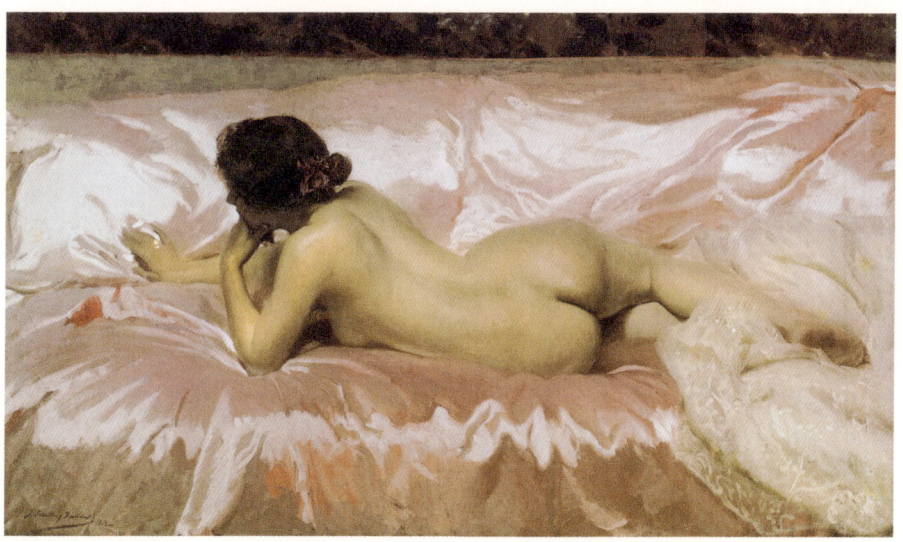

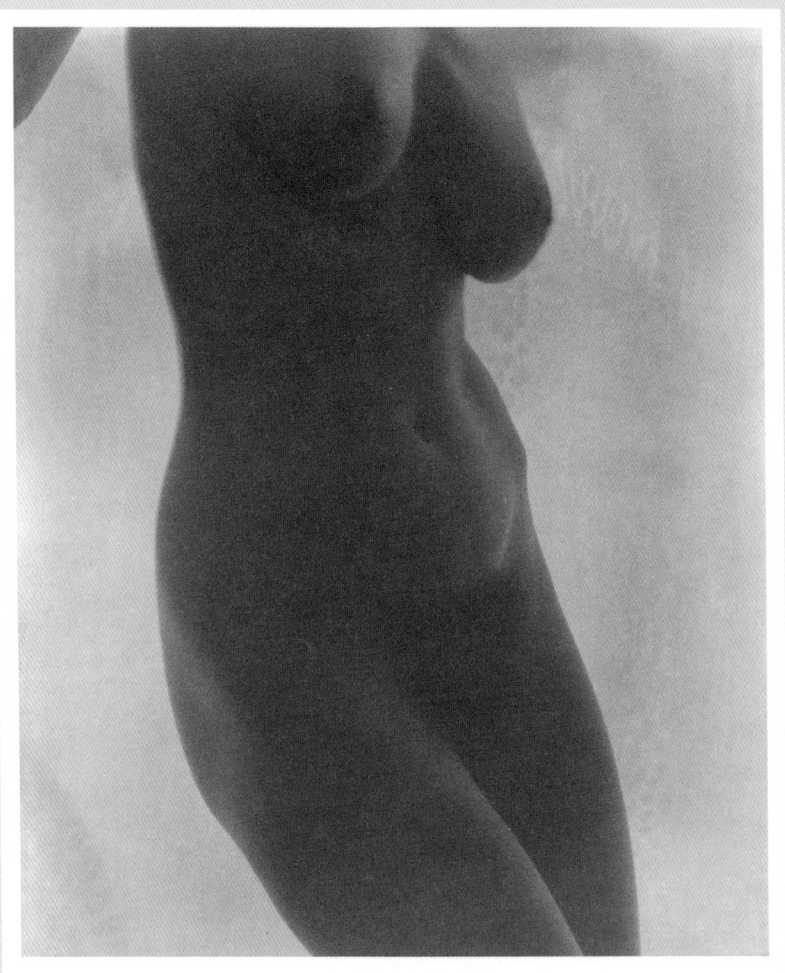

Georgia O'Keeffe, Alfred Stieglitz, 1918

Love in Close-Up

Georgia O'Keeffe & Alfred Stieglitz

There's no doubt that it was her art which initially attracted Alfred Stieglitz (1864–1946) to Georgia O'Keeffe (1887–1986). The two met in May 1916, when he included some of her work in a group show at his New York art gallery. At the time, she was an unknown 28-year-old artist. He was 52, a famous photographer and – through the exhibitions he put on at 291 Fifth Avenue – one of America's leading tastemakers in avant-garde art. But the personal chemistry between them soon began to fizz, especially when, in 1917, he hosted her first solo show. In a letter to her dated 1 June, he wrote: 'How I wanted to photograph you – the hands – the mouth – & eyes – & the enveloped in black body – the touch of white – & the throat –'.[3]

He didn't have long to wait. O'Keeffe started to pose for him almost immediately. He began by focusing on studies of her hands, but within a few months she was posing nude. He photographed her with what she called 'a kind of heat' and it was the beginning of an extraordinarily intense love affair. Between 1918 and 1937 they produced more than 350 mounted photographs; a series which The Metropolitan Museum in New York describes as having 'no equal in American art' in its 'physical scope, primal sensuality, and psychological power.'[4]

These two examples were both made in 1918. In one (opposite), the hands which Stieglitz admired so intensely interlock in a sort of balletic pose as O'Keeffe clasps her collar close about her chin. The intimacy is intensified by the close cropping of her face and, right at the centre of the composition, deep shadows emphasize the shape of her lips. If that photograph is all about O'Keeffe's hands and face, the nude (on p32) is depersonalized, like the headless remnant of a Roman sculpture. Shot against a lightly curtained window, her torso seems suspended in space. Cast mainly in shadow, just a few subtle highlights of filtered sunlight catch the top of her breast, her stomach and hip. The image seems to hold a delicate balance between eroticism, objectification and abstraction.

However, both photographs represent only part of the picture Stieglitz wanted to create. Looking back at them in 1978, O'Keeffe underlined the serial nature of the project: 'his idea of a portrait was not just one picture ... [but] a photographic diary.' [5] Given her own powerful visual imagination, they must also be seen as a collaboration between photographer and model, and a record of their relationship at the time. 'All I want is to preserve that wonderful something which so purely exists between us,' said Stieglitz in 1918. [6]

That 'wonderful something' developed into a complex affair which lasted until Stieglitz's death in 1946. He divorced his first wife and he and Georgia were married in 1924. The relationship did not remain exclusive, though – both had affairs, and for much of the time they lived apart. But they remained deeply committed to each other – some 7,000 letters survive as an enduring testament to their obsessive communication.

But what can O'Keeffe's paintings tell us about their love – or about love in general? It turns out to be a controversial question. She painted few portraits, but among the landscapes, flower paintings and imagery of shells, bones and skulls that dominate her oeuvre, are a significant number of works which seem to explore female sexuality in an extraordinarily profound

Georgia O'Keeffe, Alfred Stieglitz, 1918

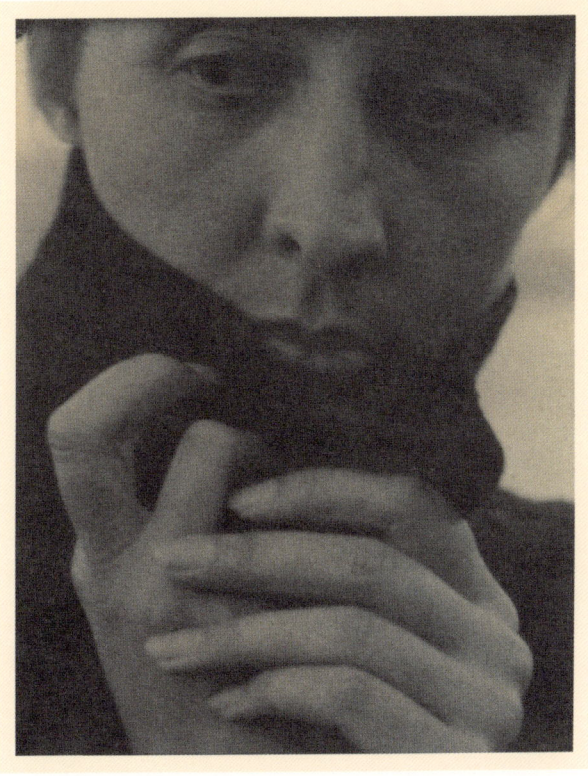

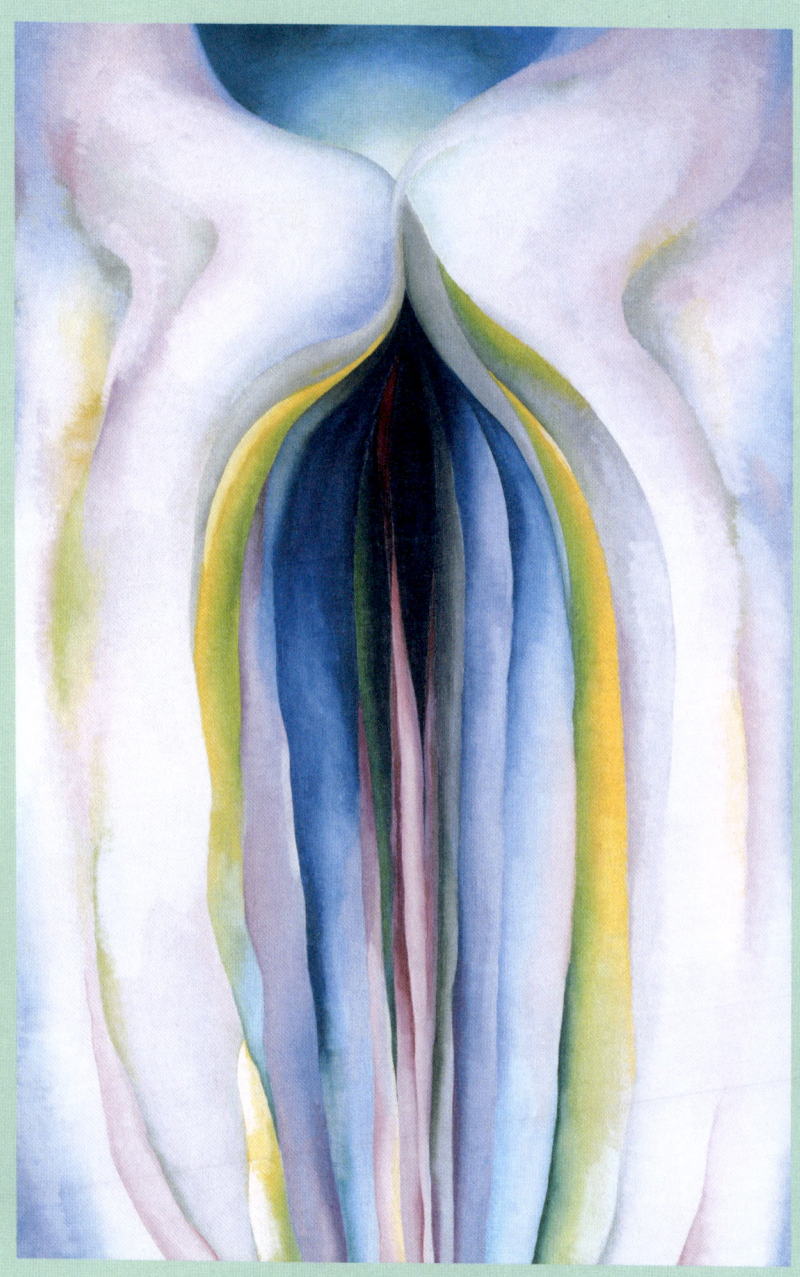

and intimate – though always indirect – way. The paintings were usually made on a large scale – much bigger than real life. As with *Grey Lines with Black, Blue and Yellow*, which she made during the heat of her relationship with Stieglitz in about 1923, they tend to focus on the inner folds, petals and delicate stamen of a single exotic bloom or tropical shell. The forms are often simplified and depicted in vibrant colours.

The visual resonances meant that many of these paintings have often been, and still are, seen as referencing the female anatomy. O'Keeffe herself was angered and frustrated by what she felt was the reductive approach of many contemporary male critics who focused on what they perceived as the sexual connotations of her art – either in a censorious or salacious way. It is likely that they were emboldened because, although Stieglitz had done much to promote her work, his photographs of O'Keeffe – in which she was a willing participant – also presented her publicly as an erotic model, sometimes even posing in front of her own paintings.

She pushed back at these one-dimensional interpretations of her own work, however, consistently denying that her pictures were intended to have sexual overtones. Certainly, they are far more complicated than that and clearly her subjects fascinated O'Keeffe as natural phenomena in their own right: 'Each shell was a beautiful world in itself,' she wrote.[7]

Despite her denials, it is hard not to see at least some of these paintings as an invitation to intimacy, even if you limit that intimacy to the private parts of a flower or a shell. And perhaps a century after they were made it doesn't seem so reductive to argue she had found a genuinely innovative way to explore and communicate female sexuality without depicting the human body. It could be seen as a new visual language which sidestepped the male gaze and the voyeuristic pleasure that female nudity had traditionally enjoyed in the longer history of art, a perspective which so obviously dominates Stieglitz's photographs of his lover.[8]

The Turkish Bath, Sylvia Sleigh, 1973

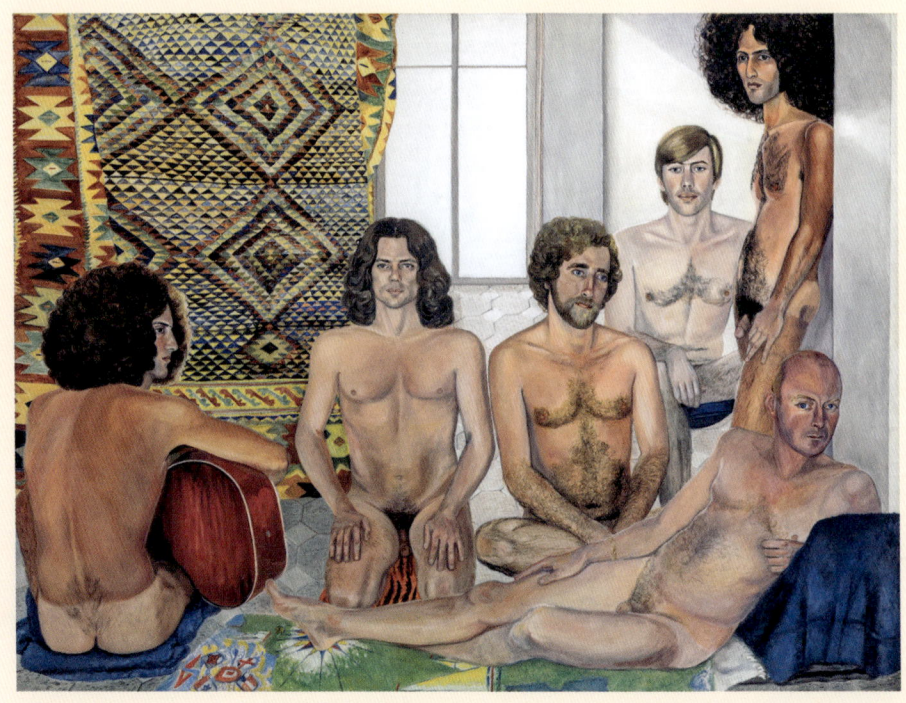

Role Reversal

Sylvia Sleigh & Lawrence Alloway

Six naked men kneeling, sitting, lounging in a sun-filled room with brilliantly coloured Turkish kilims hanging in the background. What can a picture like this tell us about love? The first barrier, for many at least, is to reset our own expectations. One of the most deeply embedded conventions in Western painting (and probably most other cultures) is that men are the watchers and women are the watched – especially when it comes to erotic art. It is male predilections which have determined how women should pose, what must be their ideal body shapes and what they should wear – or not wear.

It is not a universal rule. The male nude also has a long tradition. But for the most part when men are depicted naked, they are nearly always portrayed either as historic figures (such as Adam – see p124) or in powerful, active poses – not as vulnerable individuals, reclining suggestively. Which is why *The Turkish Bath*, by the British artist, Sylvia Sleigh (1916–2010), still has the power to disrupt our assumptions more than 50 years after she made it in 1973.

The composition shares its title with, and is a riposte to, a famous painting by the 19th-century French artist, Jean-Auguste-Dominique Ingres (1780–1867) in 1862. Depicting two dozen naked women lounging voluptuously in a bathhouse, it encapsulates the concept of the male gaze. Ingres gives us a voyeur's view of the women arranged in a multiplicity of provocative poses. It is as though he has captured them visually and presented them to us (an audience of men) as a harem from which to take our pick. It is not entirely clear how he expected women to react to it. He probably gave the matter little thought.

The fantasy goes beyond choice and availability. Ingres, who specialized in clean lines, flawless skin and elegant forms, has idealized the women. He was not interested in the reality of human form (he considered anatomy a 'dreadful science that I cannot think of without disgust') and would distort the body, and in particular female bodies, to create whatever curve or sinuous line pleased him most.

Yet while the potential for lust is here, there is no love. There cannot be, because the women in Ingres' painting are not real people: they are figures of fantasy – 'unindividuated houris',[9] as Sleigh once called them. Her approach to her own version of *The Turkish Bath* was fundamentally different. She had several different priorities. She was staking a claim for equality between female and male artists, she was campaigning for women to have the right to see and enjoy male nudes – to express their own physical desire – and she was protesting against the deeply embedded culture of the objectification of women.

She was also reacting against objectification in general. The men in this painting – and the many other nudes that she depicted – are not idealizations: they are her friends. The guitarist, for example, is the musician, Paul Rosano, and the kneeling figure is the artist and critic, Scott Burton. 'I painted them as portraits, not as sex objects, but sympathetically as intelligent and admired people,'[10] she said.

That is where the love comes in – Sleigh's painting does not tell us only about female desire and the male gaze. It also tells us about her feelings for the writer and curator, Lawrence Alloway (1926–1990). He is the figure depicted lying in the foreground. His pose derives partly from Ingres' painting, but

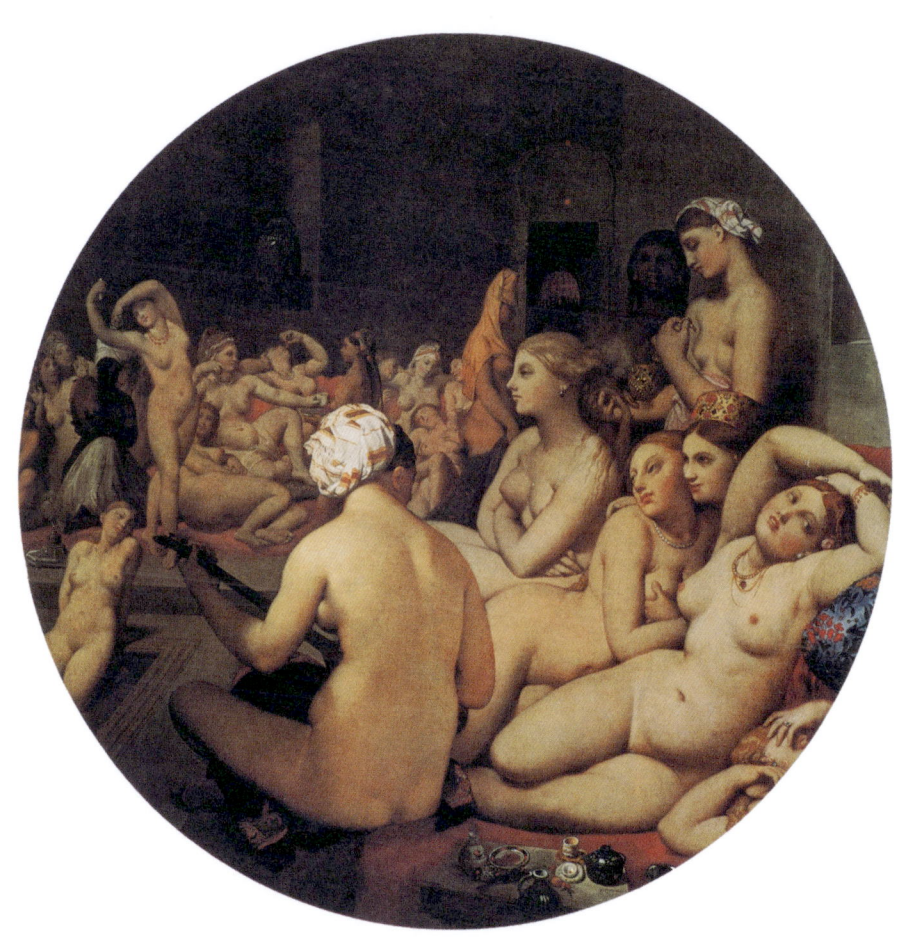

The Turkish Bath, Jean-Auguste-Dominique Ingres, 1862

Is this just coincidence or does it represent a spark of love and desire?

also from some of the most famous female nudes in art history – Manet's *Olympia*, for example, and the reclining Venuses painted by Titian in the 16th century. (There are, perhaps, echoes of Shocking Blue's song, 'Venus', which had been number one in America two years earlier: 'I'm your Venus, I'm your fire, at your desire?')

Of all the six men, Alloway is the one who engages most directly with the viewer. He meets our gaze with a particular intensity and the maritime symbols on the beach towel he is lying on are – some have suggested – evocative of traditional images of the birth of Venus (see p170). On top of this, Sleigh has positioned him so that his heel rests in the centre of a compass rose – which radiates out like a sunburst. Is this just coincidence or does it represent a spark of love and desire?

By 1973, when the painting was made, Alloway and Sleigh had been lovers for many years. They had met at an art history evening class at the University of London in 1943 when she was still with her first husband. He was only 17 at the time, she was 27. But a deep emotional and intellectual connection developed between them and they married in 1954, moving seven years later to New York City. Here Sleigh became one of the founders of the all-women SOHO20 gallery and a pioneer of feminist art. She painted Alloway more than 30 times, fully clothed, naked and even as a bejewelled bride (*The Bride*, 1949, Tate) – another disruptive gender reversal. But *The Turkish Bath* is her most deep-felt statement of both her artistic agenda and her love for Alloway.

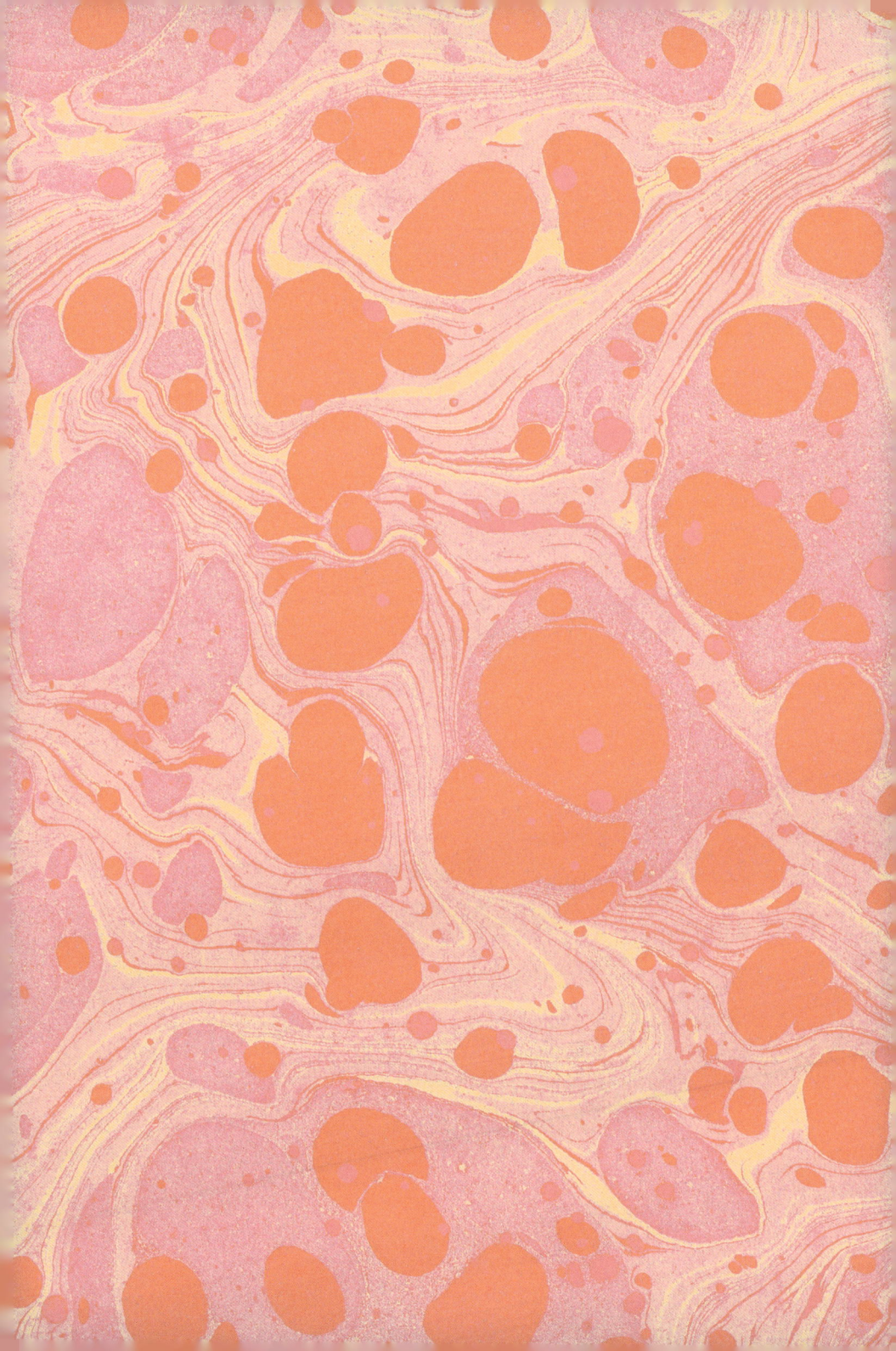

SOUL

MATES

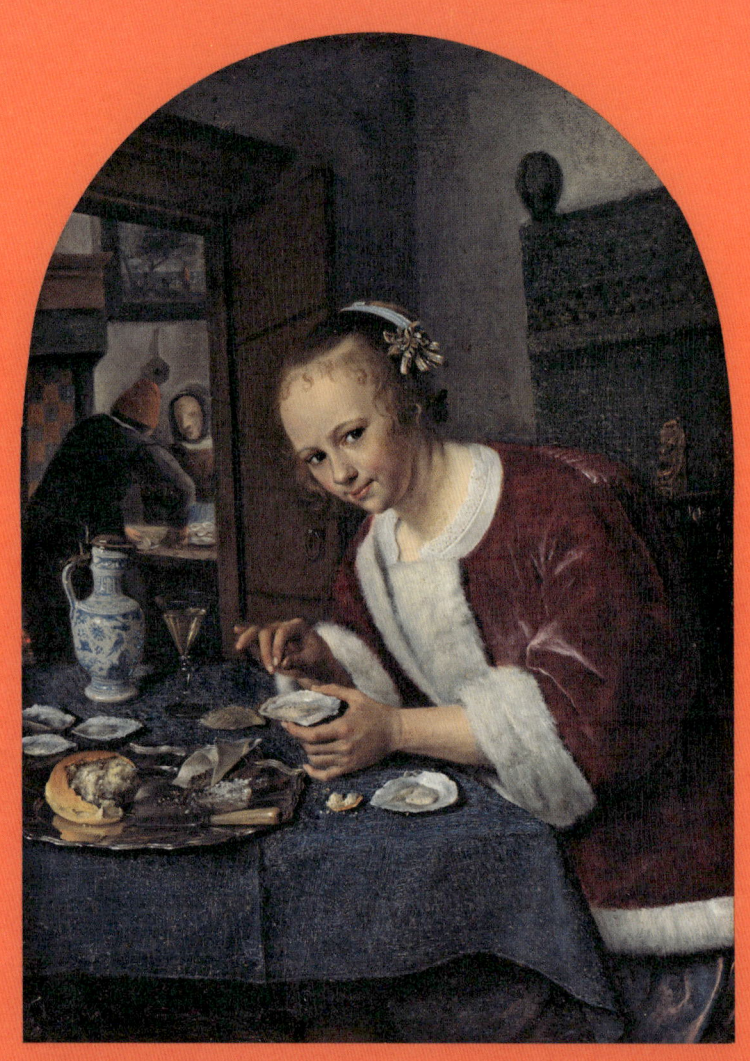

Girl Offering Oysters, Jan Steen, c.1658–1660

Perfect Harmony

Jan & Margriet Steen

Y ou can tell from his many boisterous, irreverent
paintings that Jan Steen loved to enjoy himself.
He specialized in depicting parties, tavern scenes
and chaotic households, and filling them with fun and humour,
flirtation and bawdiness. Very often the character most enjoying
all the fun is Steen himself, as he includes his own self-portrait –
always smiling or laughing – in many of his paintings. As a lute
player, a rogue, a fool, a general comic troublemaker or – as, in
fact, he was also in real life – a jovial innkeeper.

If it is obvious that Steen loved life, it is also clear that
he loved his wife. While he included himself in many of his
paintings, he used Margriet – the daughter of Steen's teacher,
Jan van Goyen – as a model even more frequently and, judging
from her expressions and the frequency of her appearances, they
both relished the collaboration.

Jan and Margriet had married in Leiden in 1649, when
he was 23 and she was probably slightly younger – and also
pregnant. They went on to have eight children, but somehow
she seems to have found time to pose for Steen on a regular basis.
Very often he placed her centre stage, looking directly at the
viewer. This is Margriet at her most flirtatious in a painting called
Girl Offering Oysters (c.1658–1660). It is a tiny picture – only

20.5cm x 14.5cm. But in this jewel-like work, Steen has captured what is surely one of the most seductive and suggestive glances in the whole of art history. If ever a woman looked at someone with love so obviously on her mind, then Margriet does so here.

But though we clearly feel the connection between artist and sitter, this was not intended as a portrait. Paintings like this were made for the open market, for the prosperous Dutch middle classes, who loved to line their walls with pictures by fashionable artists like Steen. They especially enjoyed humorous 'genre' scenes – traditional depictions of certain social situations or character types. Although most of Steen's customers would have seen themselves as respectable Calvinists, they seem to have taken enormous pleasure in being warned about moral jeopardy in the most salacious ways, safe in the knowledge perhaps that risqué scenes of bawdiness, smoking, drinking and promiscuity could be explained away as a warning against such dangerous vices.

They also enjoyed the decoding game – the visual puns and clues which the artist used to make it clear exactly what was going on. For example, oysters were considered to be aphrodisiacs, as indeed they are now: 'they arouse appetite and desire to eat and to sleep together, both of which rather appeal to lusty as well as to delicate people,' said one medical handbook published in 1651.[11] In this painting, Margriet is not only just about to eat an oyster, she is also seasoning it with a pinch of salt to make it even more irresistible. There are other signifiers associated with lust in the picture, including the wine on the table and the glowing coals in the fireplace in the next room which are warming the backside of a servant who is shucking oysters for a maid.

Of course, when he included Margriet in the frame, Steen had a get-out. He wasn't really depicting his wife as a lascivious temptress. She was simply a model. But, in practice, he was adding a new dimension to the painting, revealing and relishing the playful – and erotic – nature of his own relationship with her. And because the connection between them was real, it seems

The Music Lesson, Jan Steen, c.1650

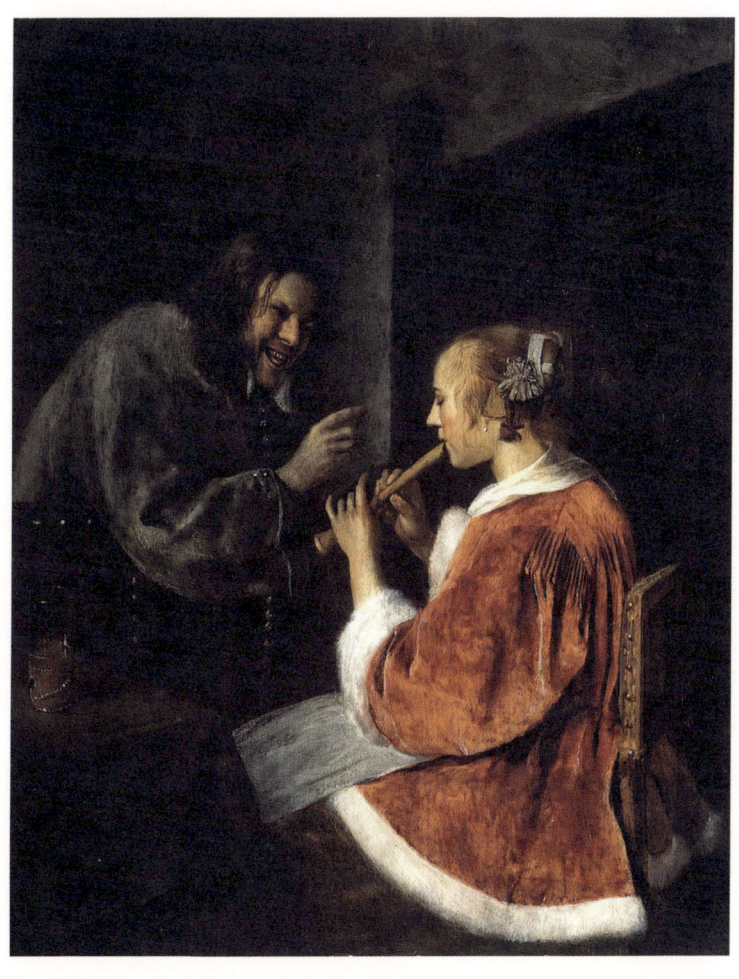

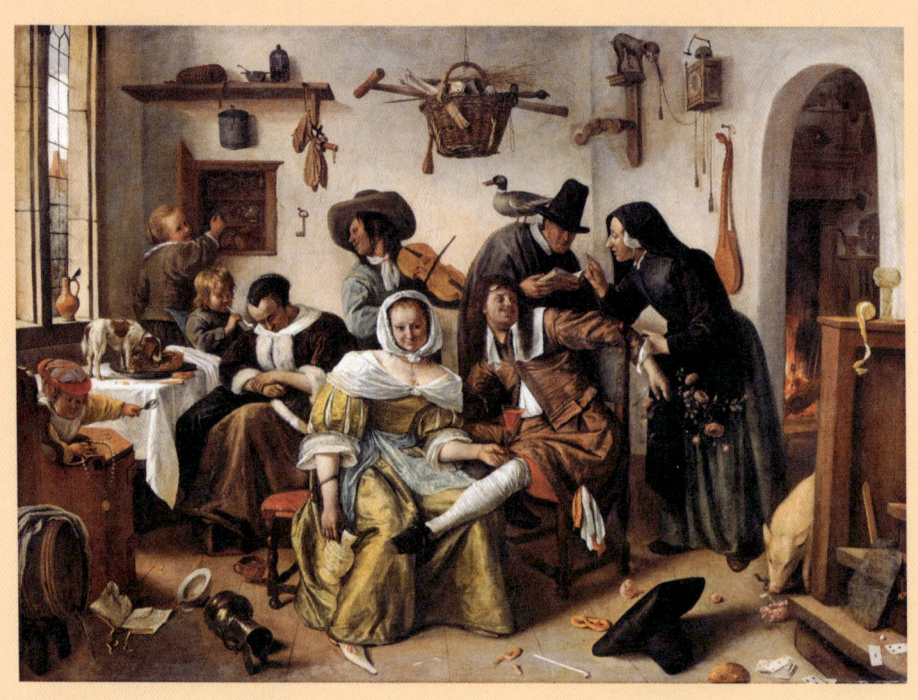

Beware of Luxury, Jan Steen, c.1663

that much more convincing and gives Steen's paintings additional charisma and force.

Perhaps the painting which pushes the boundaries most suggestively is *The Music Lesson* (c.1650) made about a year after their marriage. Steen depicts Margriet as the student and himself as the teacher. The phallic innuendo of the recorder and its position vis a vis Steen's midriff, would have been immediately understood at the time. But if we were in any doubt, Jan's lascivious grin and the glint in his eye confirms what was on his mind. The demure pose of Margriet only adds to the tension.

If there is a moral dimension to be found in *The Music Lesson*, it probably counts as a warning not to leave your wife alone with her music teacher. But the moralizing is much clearer in Steen's larger-scale paintings of chaotic, dysfunctional families for which he is still famous. *Beware of Luxury* (c.1663) is a classic example, full of chaos and jeopardy. In a topsy-turvy world, a child smokes a pipe, the dog eats the pie while the matriarch sleeps, and the baby throws his dish on the floor. And the flirtatious woman at the centre of it all, holding the wine glass so suggestively? Margriet Steen. Jan is having more affectionate fun at his wife's expense.

Sadly, though, after 20 apparently happy years of marriage, Margriet died in 1669. Jan remarried a widow called Maria four years later and included her portrait in his work for another decade. She fulfilled similar roles to Margriet, but somehow Steen doesn't conjure up quite the same erotic charisma.

There seems to be a good reason for this. Another painter once found Maria in a despondent mood. She complained that Jan depicted her 'sometimes as an indecent object, sometimes as a horny tart, sometimes as a match-maker or a drunken whore, which annoyed her ... she wished to be portrayed as a proper woman.' [12] Clearly between Jan and Maria, there wasn't quite the same chemistry, the same shared sense of humour which shines through in his paintings of Margriet.

The Birthday, Marc Chagall, 1915

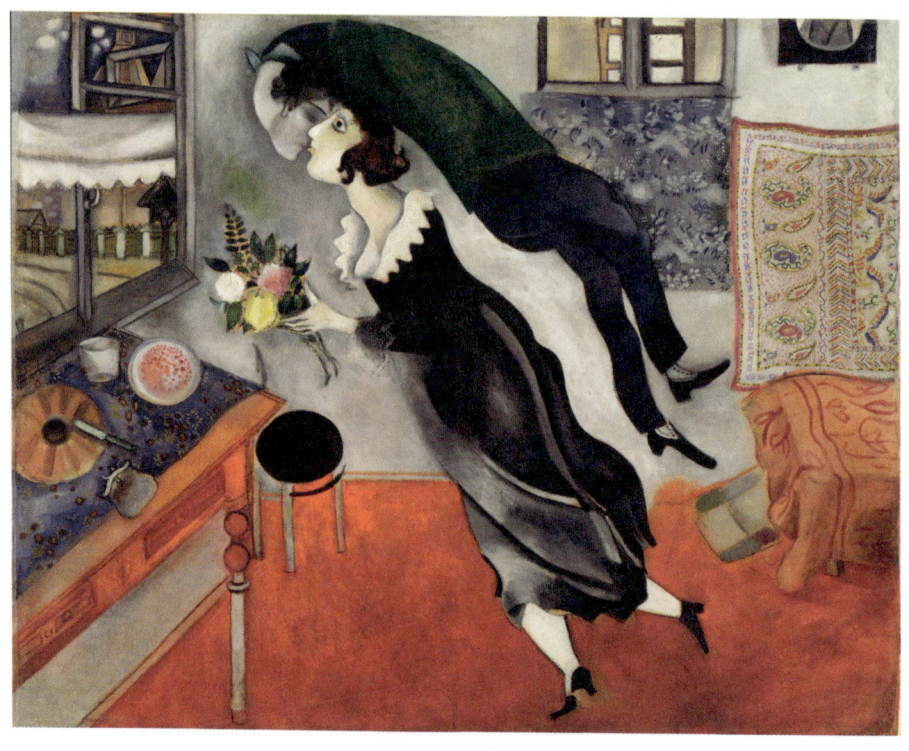

Flight of Fancy

Marc & Bella Chagall

In art it can be hard to separate fantasy from reality. And, in the surreal world of Marc Chagall (1887–1985), the two seem inextricably fused – especially when his paintings are inspired by love. *The Birthday*, which he began on his 28th birthday in July 1915, was not intended to mark that anniversary, but his marriage to Bella Rosenfeld (1895–1944) which took place a couple of weeks later.

It is typical in the heady emotion which infuses the many pictorial celebrations that Marc Chagall made of their relationship. Grasping a bunch of summery birthday flowers, Bella kicks her feet and gently lifts off the bright red floor. It is as though she is swimming weightlessly up through the air towards the open window. Chagall, body armless, back arched, cranes his impossibly elongated neck so that he meets her with a kiss. Their lips are about to touch. Bella is slightly startled, Chagall with eyes closed, enraptured.

It isn't just the two lovers who float free from reality. The picture is full of visual non sequiturs. Try following the line of the skirting board. It stops, starts and disappears into a blur, so that the walls seem to be melting into the floor. In a similar way, the blue-and-white cloth hanging behind Chagall – a Kashmiri shawl which he had given to Bella – does not re-emerge on the

Grasping a bunch of summery birthday flowers, Bella kicks her feet and gently lifts off the bright red floor.

lower side of his body. Meanwhile, Bella is depicted with a clean, flowing outline, except for the front of her dress which forms a long smudge as it appears to merge with the wall behind. Her face, too, is clearly defined, but her bright wide-staring eyes contrast with Chagall's shadowy features just behind her cheek. The stool and the table and utensils laid on it are also angled awkwardly, ignoring the rules of perspective and adding to our sense of disorientation. In short, like many of Chagall's paintings, it is an image from the theatre of dreams: gentle, tender dreams in a giddy world where lovers kiss and flowers bloom, but gravity and normal perspective no longer apply.

Interestingly, the way the two lovers wrote about their relationship slipped into a similar language of reverie. This is Marc's description of their first meeting in their home town of Vitebsk, Belarus, in 1909: 'I feel she has known me always, my childhood, my present life, my future; as if she were watching over me, divining my innermost being'.[13]

In Bella's version of the same event, she claims to have a premonition of love even before she actually sees him and then a sense of weightlessness as they part: 'A shadow darkened the chink in the doorway ... I felt as if something were scorching me. Light spread over the walls, and against them appeared the face of a boy, as white as the walls ... I was floating back up to the cloud. His cloud. I fell into a long sleep. I began to live a new life'.[14]

When that new life began, both were living in the Jewish community in Vitebsk. Chagall was an aspiring 22-year-old artist from a poor family, while Bella's parents were wealthy jewellers. The meeting plunged them into a world from which, in his art, Chagall never quite seems to emerge. His lifelong love affair with Bella became a dominant theme in his paintings.

Few of the many hundreds of pictures and sketches he made which include representations or references to Bella could be called portraits, however. When she appears, often in a dream-like setting, we know it is her, from her calm, impassive expression and her dark hair, but we get little sense of her character. What matters to Chagall is not that we understand her, but that we understand the effect she has on him.

Despite the nostalgia and the reverie of their painted world, reality for the Chagalls was often challenging. Together with their daughter Ida, who was born almost exactly nine months after their wedding night, their togetherness was often threatened by war and revolution and the apocalyptic antisemitic persecution that benighted Europe during the Nazi era. Indeed, as Chagall's biographer has pointed out, pictures which so obviously encapsulate love and peace were recast by the Nazis as 'green, purple, and red Jews shooting out of the earth, fiddling on violins, flying through the air, cumulatively representing a Jewish catastrophe and assault on Western civilisation'.[15]

The family only just managed to escape from France to America in 1941 but, three years later, Bella died from a throat infection. Chagall stopped painting for nine months as he and Ida immersed themselves in translating and illustrating Bella's memoirs (written originally in Yiddish). When he finally set up his easel again, it was to create *Around Her*, an image of Vitebsk glowing under a magical moon is delivered as though in a vision by an angel. Chagall's head has become inverted and is it Ida or Bella who weeps with him? We can't be sure. The two lovers are flying still, however, soaring together into the night. But the flowers have become a wreath and Bella's wedding train has become the brilliant white trail of a comet.

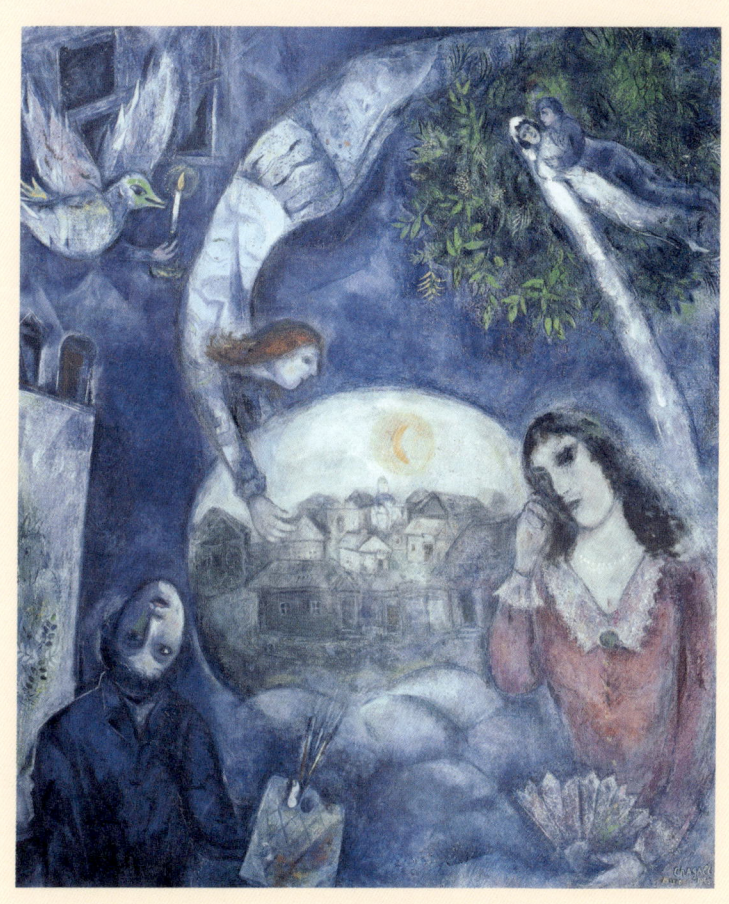

Around Her, Marc Chagall, 1945

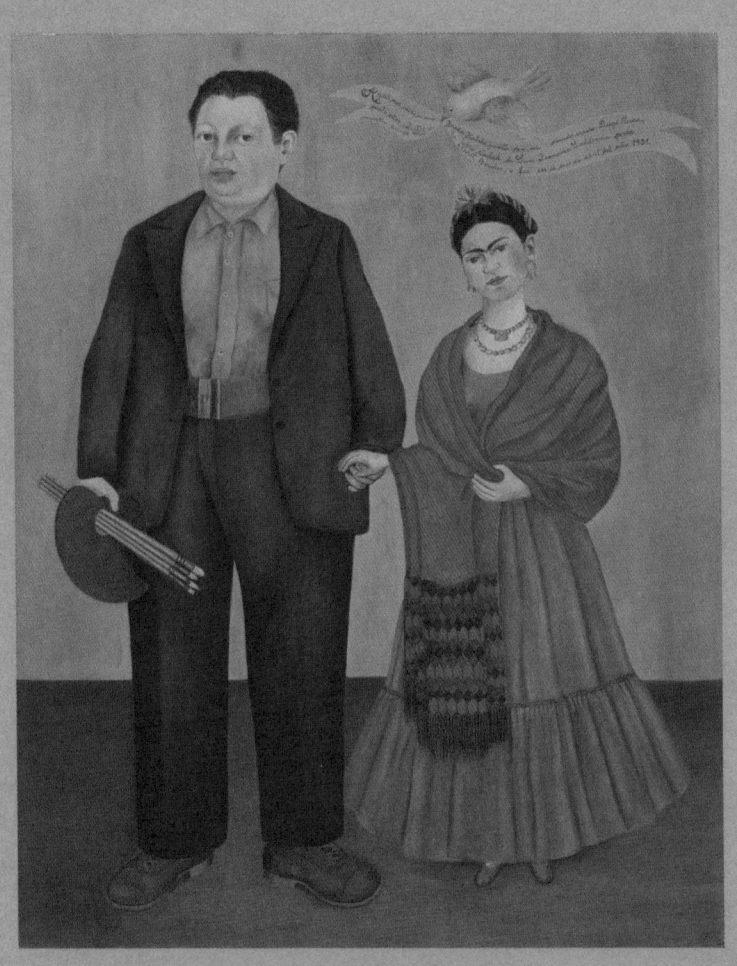

Frida and Diego Rivera, Frida Kahlo, 1931

Mind Games

Frida Kahlo & Diego Rivera

'Here you see us, me Frida Kahlo, together with my beloved husband Diego Rivera'.[16] That is the beginning of the intriguing inscription on the banner delivered by the dove in Frida Kahlo's double portrait which she made in 1931, two years after the couple married. It is intriguing because, although it ostensibly celebrates their togetherness, it also emphasizes that they are individuals, and that sense of separateness is reflected in the image itself.

The two are depicted in their own separate spaces, barely touching. It is painted by Frida, yet it shows Rivera as the artist, palette and brushes in hand. They are clean and apparently unused, however, and it is Frida in her bright red shawl and deep green dress who provides the colour in the picture. The way they hold hands is strange too. The fingers do not interlock in a lovers' grasp. She places hers gently to cover his upturned fingertips.

Kahlo (1907–1954) also does nothing to mask the discrepancy in their physical size. Rivera – a huge man – was six foot one and weighed more than 21 stone; Kahlo was five foot three and weighed about seven stone. The effect is that they look more like a father and his dutiful daughter than passionate lovers.

Perhaps this sense of separateness, even at this early stage in their married life, stems from Frida's uncertainties about the forces which were already beginning to come between them. Despite the intense emotional chemistry which bound them together, the relationship was always turbulent and there were frequent rows. The couple were at the epicentre of artistic and radical political circles in Mexico City. Each had their own powerful sexual charisma and their marriage was never monogamous. Rivera was regularly unfaithful, including with Kahlo's own sister, Cristina. Frida had her own lovers too, both male and female, including Leon Trotsky, who was staying with them in Mexico City during his exile from the Soviet Union, and – allegedly – Georgia O'Keeffe and Josephine Baker. Tensions between Kahlo and Rivera often came to the surface and ultimately led to divorce in 1939. But such was the deep bond between them that they remarried less than a year later.

That bond is evoked in a painting which Frida began during that year of separation, although it wasn't completed until 1943. In her *Self-Portrait as a Tehuana*, she depicts herself in the traditional Tehuana costume worn by the Zapotec women from Tehuantepec in the Oaxaca region of Mexico, which was her mother's homeland. This has symbolic force not only because it emphasizes her ethnic roots, but because Tehuantepec had a reputation as a matriarchal society which set it apart from the rest of Mexico's highly patriarchal culture.[17]

But while that tradition may give Frida a certain sense of female empowerment, the painting is a powerful expression of the fragility of her emotions and her vulnerability to Diego. Loose threads from the Tehuana headdress radiate out in all directions, as though the surface of the painting is shattering around her face, while myriad strands of her hair form subsidiary crazes across the canvas. And there, emerging from her eyebrows and imprinted on her forehead is the cause of the fractures – an image of Diego.

While Frida explored their relationship almost obsessively over the years, Rivera was much more reserved in his artistic response to their relationship. Most of his energies went into

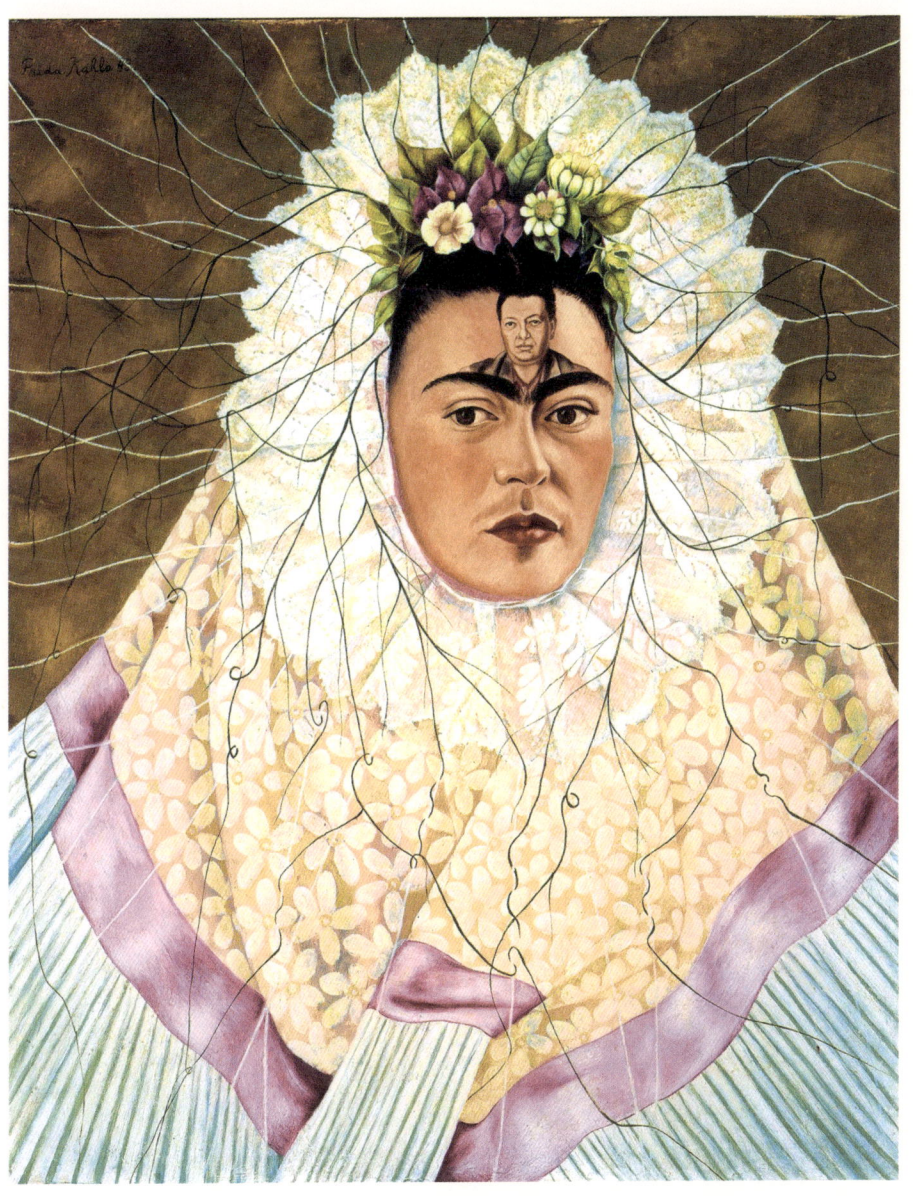

Self-Portrait as a Tehuana (or Diego on My Mind), Frida Kahlo, 1943

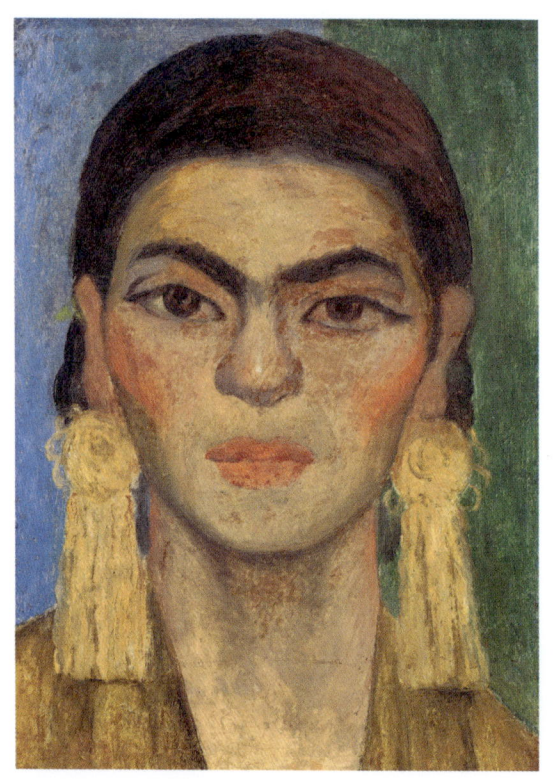

Portrait of Frida Kahlo, Diego Rivera, c.1939

large-scale murals with political and historical themes. So the tiny
size of his only-known portrait of his wife – it's just 14in x 10in –
is particularly poignant. It was made in 1935, another turbulent
year in their relationship, when he was having an affair with her
sister, Cristina. Its size reflects its jewel-like qualities: the gold
earrings, so prominent and redolent of ancient Mexican or Aztec
culture, the ruby-red lips and the background of sapphire blue
and emerald green. It seems to enforce his tribute to her art in
general which 'shines like a diamond in the very centre of a great
jewel, clear and hard, precious and cutting'.[18] The painting was
still in his studio until his death in 1957, three years after Frida
had passed away.

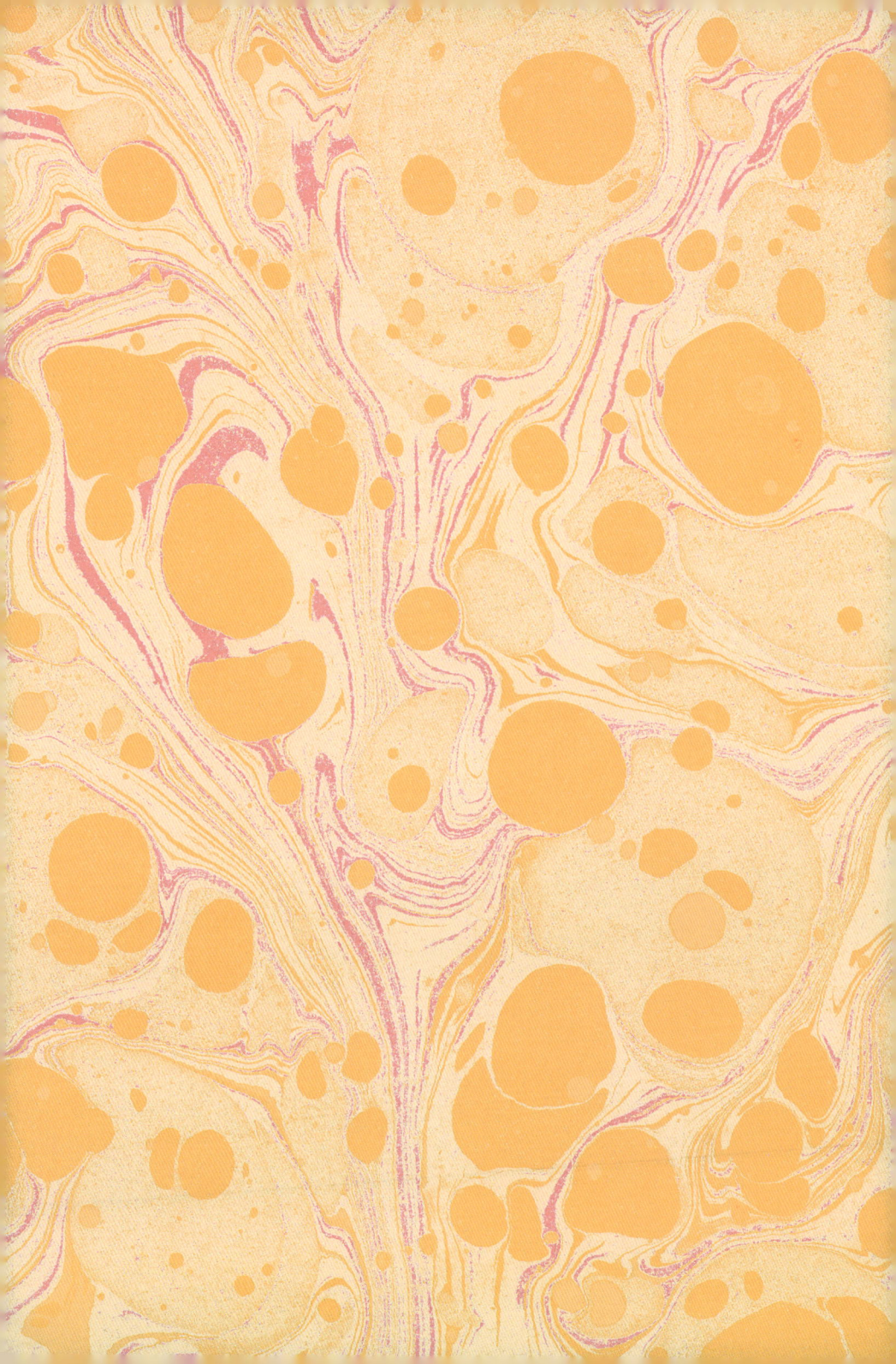

SECRET

AFFAIRS

Unconventional Love

Filippo Lippi & Lucrezia Buti

'Fra Filippo was so lustful that he would give anything to enjoy a woman he wanted if he thought he could have his way; and if he couldn't buy what he wanted, then he would cool his passion by painting her portrait and reasoning with himself.' [19]

This description of Filippo Lippi (1406–1469) by Giorgio Vasari (1511–1574) was written two generations after Lippi's death. But it is backed up by plenty of contemporary evidence that he was an impetuous man with a voracious appetite for the pleasures of life (despite the fact that he had, at one time, taken holy orders to be a friar). But Vasari's idea that he could cool, rather than inflame, his passion by painting a woman's portrait is a misguided one. Much more likely, Lippi persuaded women he fancied to sit as models and, rather than reason his way out of his lust, seized the opportunity to seduce them.

That seems to be what happened when, in 1456, he was asked to make a painting by some nuns in Prato. He agreed on the condition that a particular novice nun – the 20-year-old Lucrezia Buti (c.1435–c.1500) – would sit as a model for the Virgin Mary. We can only assume that his reason failed and his lust was inflamed, as he promptly abducted not only her, but her sister too, and then incarcerated them in his house.

Although this all happened nearly 600 years ago, the bones of the story seem to be reliable. The 'abduction' was probably consensual and the attraction between nun and artist mutual. A son, Filippino, who became an artist in his own right, was born, probably in 1457, and they had a daughter, Alessandra, in 1465.

The most fascinating insight into their relationship is in Lippi's art – and, most notably, in the *Madonna and Child with Two Angels*, one of his greatest masterpieces. It seems, at first glance, the most calm, serene and harmonious of images. A demure Virgin Mary prays with eyes downcast, while a highly naturalistic baby reaches out towards her, supported by two angels.

The illusionistic set-up of the painting is highly unusual and inventive. Mary sits on a throne whose arm projects out towards us. The throne seems to be placed in front of a window overlooking a distant landscape. Yet our perceptions are confused and surely deliberately so. The window frame looks more like a picture frame and its outline coincides exactly with the edges of the window. So maybe it isn't a window at all – perhaps this is a picture within a picture?

What has all this got to do with love? There is a long tradition that the painting represents Lucrezia, and possibly also their first child, Filippino, in the guise of the angel looking slightly mischievously towards the viewer. Some art historians baulk at the long tradition that identifies Lippi's Madonnas with Lucrezia. But several other paintings of the Virgin by Lippi made after he had met Lucrezia seem to have been posed by the same woman, with fine delicate features and grey-brown eyes.

These paintings – and especially the *Madonna and Child with Two Angels* – have a particular intensity to them and it surely makes sense that he would have asked his beautiful young partner to sit for him. Her pose also offers an interesting psychological insight: despite the sense of serenity, if we look closely at Mary's body position, it is not quite decorous. The angel

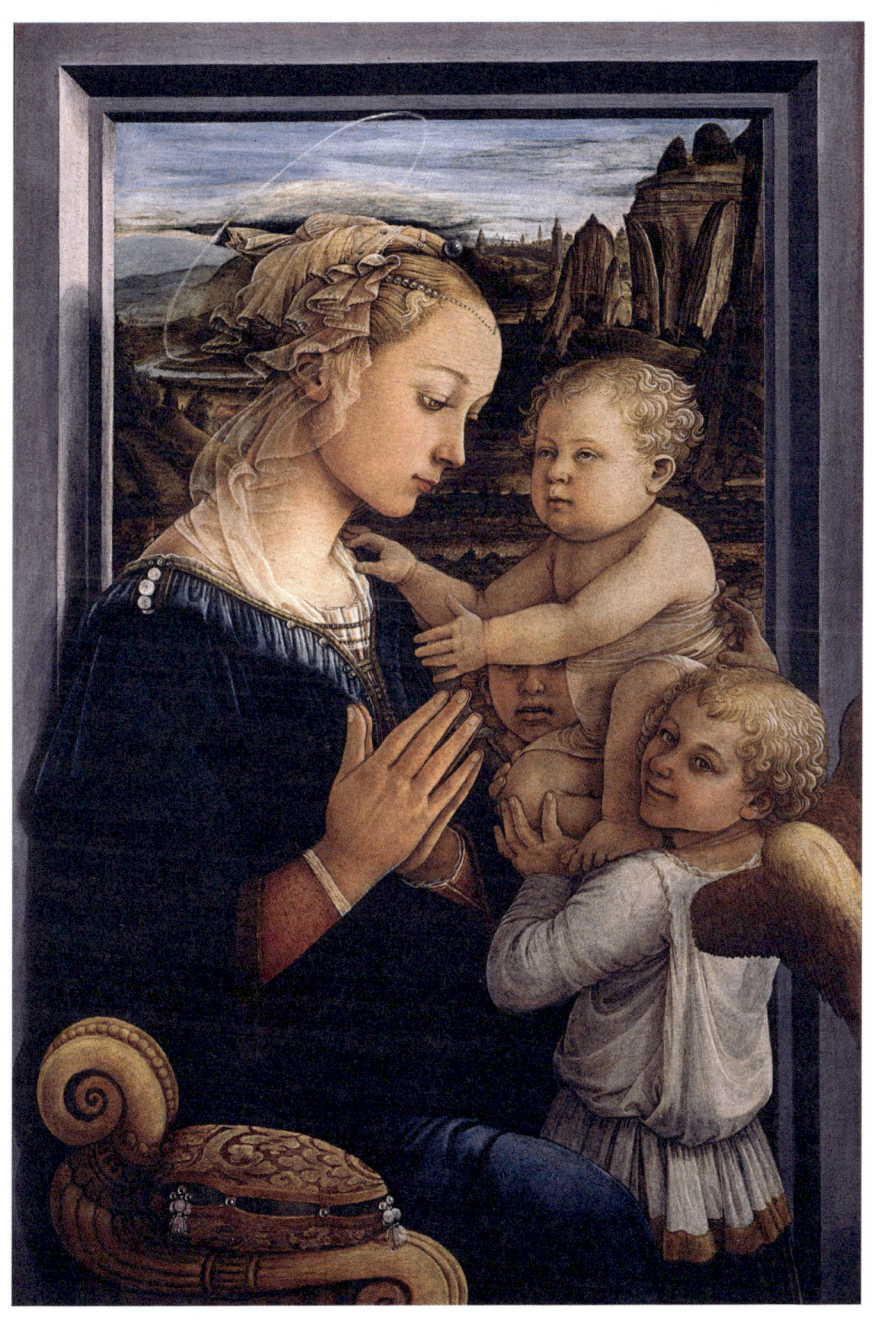

Madonna and Child with Two Angels, Filippo Lippi, 1460–1465

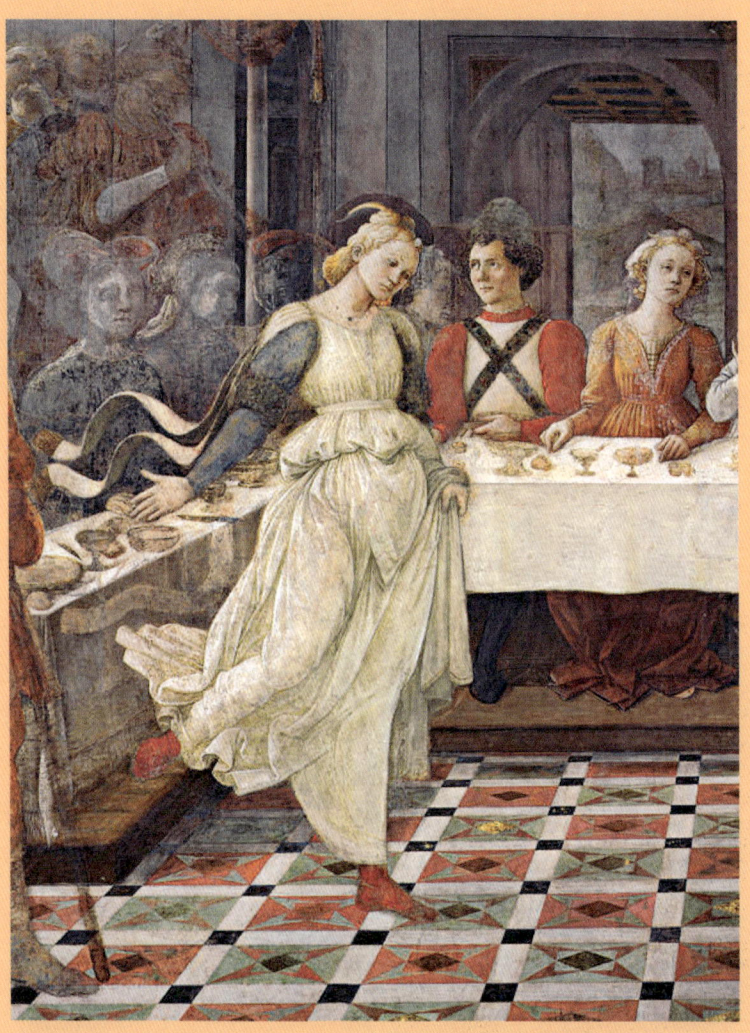

Salome Dancing (detail) from *Scenes from the Life of
Saint John the Baptist: Herod's Feast*, Filippo Lippi, 1452–1465

in the foreground is standing directly between her legs, so that her right knee opens out towards us in a slightly suggestive way. It's almost as though Fra Lippi couldn't quite stop his mind from meandering a little.

Lippi didn't depict Lucrezia only as the Virgin. At one point, early in their relationship, he wandered into more salacious territory. In his commission to depict the *Stories of Saint Stephen and Saint John the Baptist* in fresco in Prato cathedral, he seems to have persuaded Lucrezia to model for the figure of Salome dancing at Herod's feast. In the Bible, Herod promised to grant his beautiful step-daughter, Salome, any request if she would dance for him. Once the dance was done, prompted by her mother, Herodias, she demanded the head of John the Baptist, whom Herod had incarcerated but didn't want to kill. However, he was bound to keep his word and, as a result, Salome was seen both as a totem of eroticism and a symbol of the dangers of unbridled lust – especially of an older man for a younger woman.

Was the 50-year-old Lippi's depiction of Lucrezia as Salome a wry reflection of her erotic power over him? It is tempting to think so. Certainly Salome's dance, which takes centre stage in the fresco, is – for its day and considering its setting in a church – highly suggestive. She holds her skirts with one hand, revealing her bright red slippers, and raises her other arm and leg in what seems to be the beginnings of a spin. That probably didn't do much to cool Fra Lippi's ardour.[20]

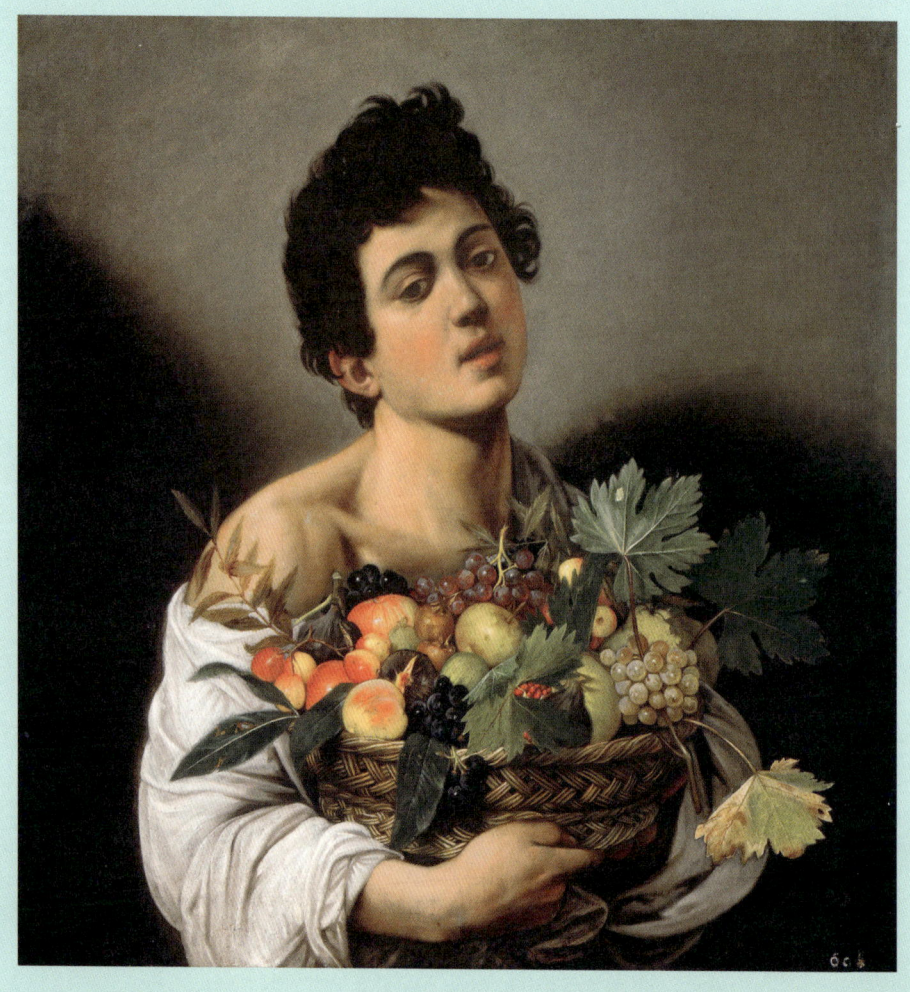

Love Without Fear

Caravaggio

A youth – perhaps in his late teens – stares directly at us over a cornucopia of autumn fruit. The basket is so full that he clutches it to his chest to avoid it spilling. His gaze is languorous, his cheeks flushed, his full red lips are parted and his tunic has fallen from his shoulder. A beam of sunlight from an unseen window above his head creates dramatic highlights on his face, neck and hand. There are no distractions in the background, just deep shadows. He feels real, not trapped by the two-dimensional plane of the picture, but close to us, part of our space. That, combined with his stare and the slight lift of his chin, creates a powerful intimacy – he seems to be simultaneously inviting and challenging the viewer. Meanwhile, we can't avoid the suggestive overtones: the fruit speaks of voluptuousness. A ripe fig has split at the base; behind a vine leaf, a pomegranate has cracked open and spilt its seed; someone has plucked a grape from the bunch which hangs over the front of the basket.

This was one of the first paintings made by Michelangelo Merisi da Caravaggio after he arrived in Rome from Milan in 1592. He was just 21, an impoverished but brilliantly promising artist who was still scratching a living as a jobbing painter's assistant. The painting can be interpreted in many ways. It is a portrait, but also – in the basket of fruit – a still life. There may

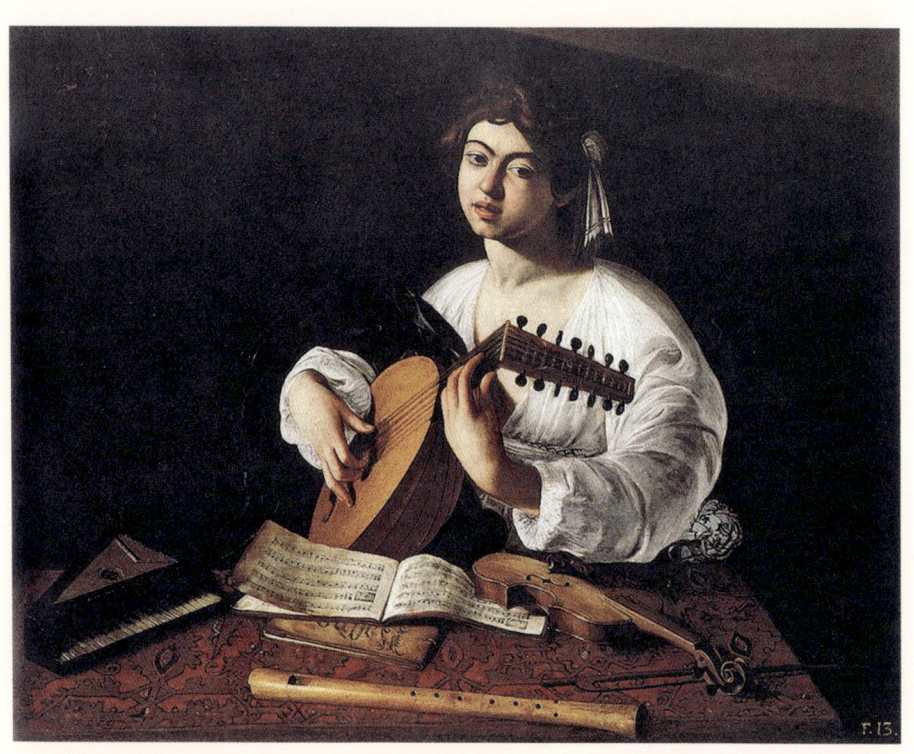

The Lute Player, Caravaggio, c.1596

be references, too, to the traditions of ancient classical painting. Above all, however, it is a showpiece, a virtuosic demonstration of the young artist's talents and the beginnings of Caravaggio's experiments with dramatic lighting effects. But whichever way we are tempted to see it, the sense of a charged atmosphere between the painter and the sitter, and the homoerotic overtones which go with that, are crystal clear.

Many scholars believe that the painting depicts the 16-year-old Mario Minniti, another aspiring artist who had made friends with and, for some years, shared lodgings with Caravaggio. We know that Caravaggio always preferred to paint from live models and he wouldn't have been able to afford to pay one. So that theory certainly makes sense. But does the sexual charge in the painting also suggest that they were lovers? It certainly feels that way.

Over recent decades, art historians have got themselves into something of a tangle arguing about Caravaggio's sexuality. Some have claimed him as a gay icon. Others seem affronted by the idea and point to evidence suggesting he had relationships with women. It seems pointless to speculate. Most likely, Caravaggio, who never married, was bisexual and it is undeniable that a significant number of his paintings reveal a powerful and sensual response to male beauty.

What we know for sure is that he lived an extraordinarily tempestuous and often decadent life. In those early years in Rome, he spent much of his time in the backstreets – an anarchic world of brothels, taverns and gambling dens. He fell in with a wild set of young artists who lived by the motto, '*nec spe, nec metu*' ('without hope, without fear'). Pleasures must have been fleeting, often fuelled by alcohol and tempered by violence. Street fights and stabbings were common and Caravaggio himself had several run-ins with the law, finally fleeing the city in 1606 after he killed a man in a brawl.

Yet Caravaggio also lived the high life. By 1596 he had started to sell paintings and his astonishing talent was spotted by three of the richest and most important art collectors in Rome, including two cardinals. Through them, he was sucked into a hedonistic world of extreme luxury, privilege and refinement. The result was paintings like *The Lute Player*, three versions of which were made for his patrons. It probably represents an allegory of the pleasures and beauties of music, but also of love. The music so prominently displayed in the foreground was a setting for love madrigals. Probably depicting the famous castrato singer who was living in the household of Cardinal del Monte (one of his most important patrons), it is another of several examples of Caravaggio's talent and interest in languorous celebration of the beauty of male youth.

He also included himself in that cast, notably in a depiction of Bacchus, the god of pleasure and drunkenness, which he made in 1596, also probably for Del Monte. This image is almost certainly based on a self-portrait and one in which he appears as the tempter. His eyes are slightly sly, his head tilted. As with the earlier painting of Minniti, Caravaggio's gown exposes his chest and shoulder and he also includes a basket of fruit in the foreground. With one hand he offers us wine, with the other, he toys with the belt that holds the gown in place. As for the fruit, some of it is overripe and has started to rot. Perhaps, in his mind, a note of dissolution has begun to taint the pleasures of love.

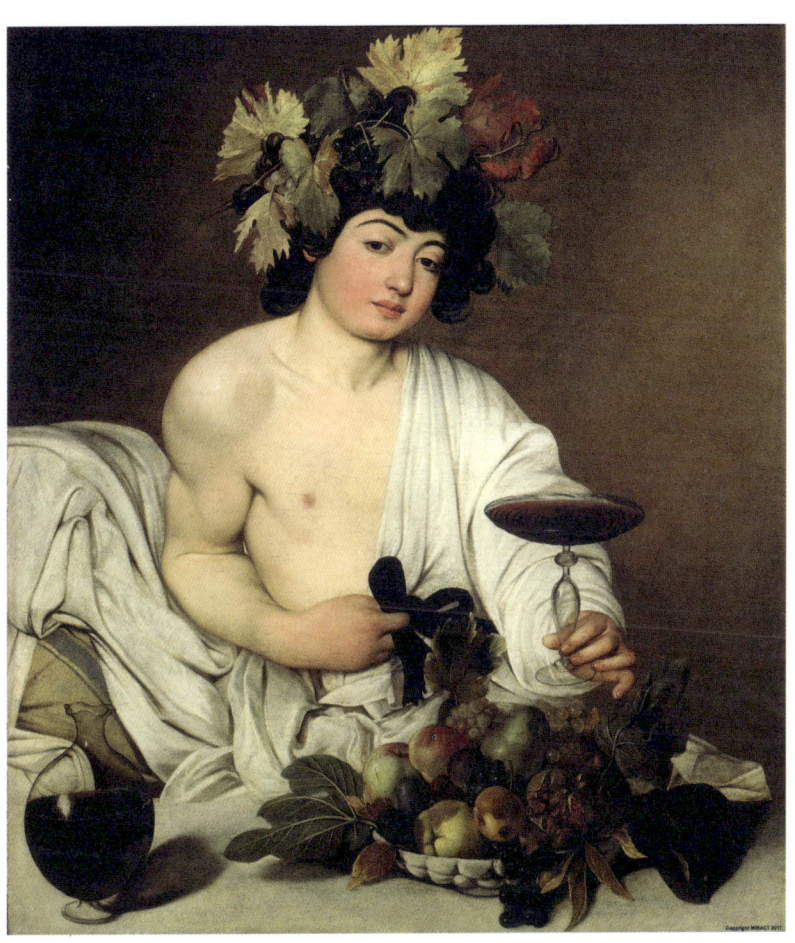

Bacchus, Caravaggio, c.1596

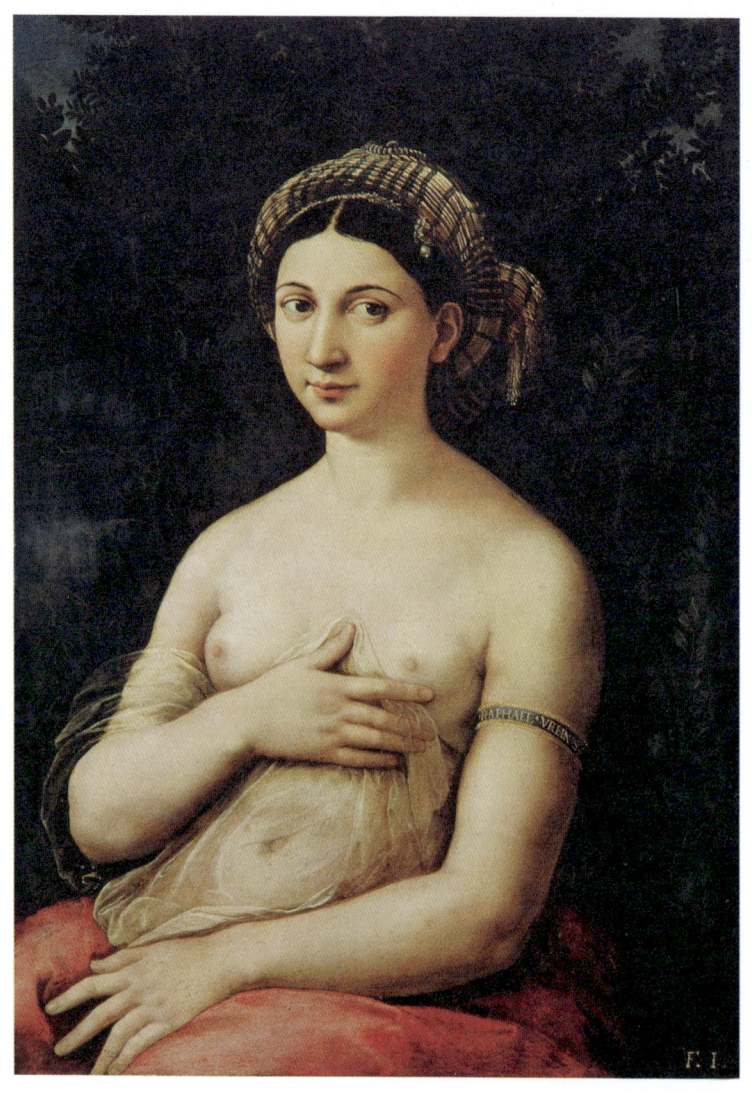

The Portrait of a Young Woman (La Fornarina), Raphael, c.1516

Mystery Lover

Raphael & Margherita Luti

A beautiful young woman, half-naked, with the very faintest of smiles flickering on her lips, looks slightly past us, not quite catching our eye. She holds a transparent, diaphanous shawl – which would in any case do very little to hide her modesty – in such a way that both her breasts are fully revealed, emphasizing rather than covering them. Her left hand is more effectively placed to conceal, but it also draws our attention to the fact that the pink fabric we see at the very bottom of the picture may only partly be covering her lap. Meanwhile, in the background to this playful game of visual hide-and-seek, is a myrtle bush – which was sacred to Venus, the goddess of love. And on the woman's arm, matching the colours of her headscarf, is a blue-and-gold band, stitched with a name – Raphael Vrbinas (Raphael of Urbino). It's at once a statement of attachment and commitment and the artist's signature.

This picture – which Raphael (1483–1520) made for his own home, not as a commission – is surely a deeply intimate and erotic portrait of his lover. Maybe she was more than a lover. Intriguingly, there is a square-cut ruby ring above the knuckle of the third finger of her left hand, which may be a sign of betrothal. Who is she? Controversy lingers,[21] but traditionally she has been known as 'la fornarina', an endearing term for a female baker, and identified as a young woman called Margherita Luti, who was the unmarried daughter of Francesco Senese, a baker from Siena. Margherita entered the convent of Sant'Apollonia soon after Raphael's death in 1520.

We will never know for sure if this is right, but the connection between artist and model is evident from the picture itself. The lack of certainty just adds to the mystique – especially when we consider the stories which circulated around Raphael's love life at the time and shortly after his death. The main source for these is Vasari, whose biographies of famous artists of the Renaissance were first written in 1550. We have to be a little careful of Vasari's accounts, which are occasionally prone to exaggeration and errors. But although he was only nine when Raphael died, Vasari did know plenty of artists who knew Raphael personally, and his account of Raphael as a man of charm, grace and boundless good nature seems to square with other reports. So when it comes to Vasari's accounts of Raphael's amorous adventures, we can safely assume that there is no smoke without fire.

And there is a lot of smoke. Raphael 'was a very amorous man' who 'secretly attended to his love affairs and pursued his amorous pleasures beyond all moderation', claims Vasari.[22] He gives the example of one patron – Agostino Chigi – who found that Raphael was so distracted by his love for his mistress that it was preventing him from working on the frescos in Chigi's villa. So he arranged for Raphael's mistress to stay in the building while he worked. This story has a ring of truth to it, but Vasari does seem to overstep the mark when he blames Raphael's death on a fever which developed from excessive sexual indulgence.

There is another intriguing dimension to Vasari's biography. Despite Raphael's philandering, and the fact that he was engaged until his sudden death intervened (his fiancée was the daughter of a cardinal – it was a political match, not a love match), there was one woman in particular whom Raphael 'loved to the day of his death'[23] and indeed provided for in his will.

Raphael 'pursued his amorous pleasures beyond all moderation'.

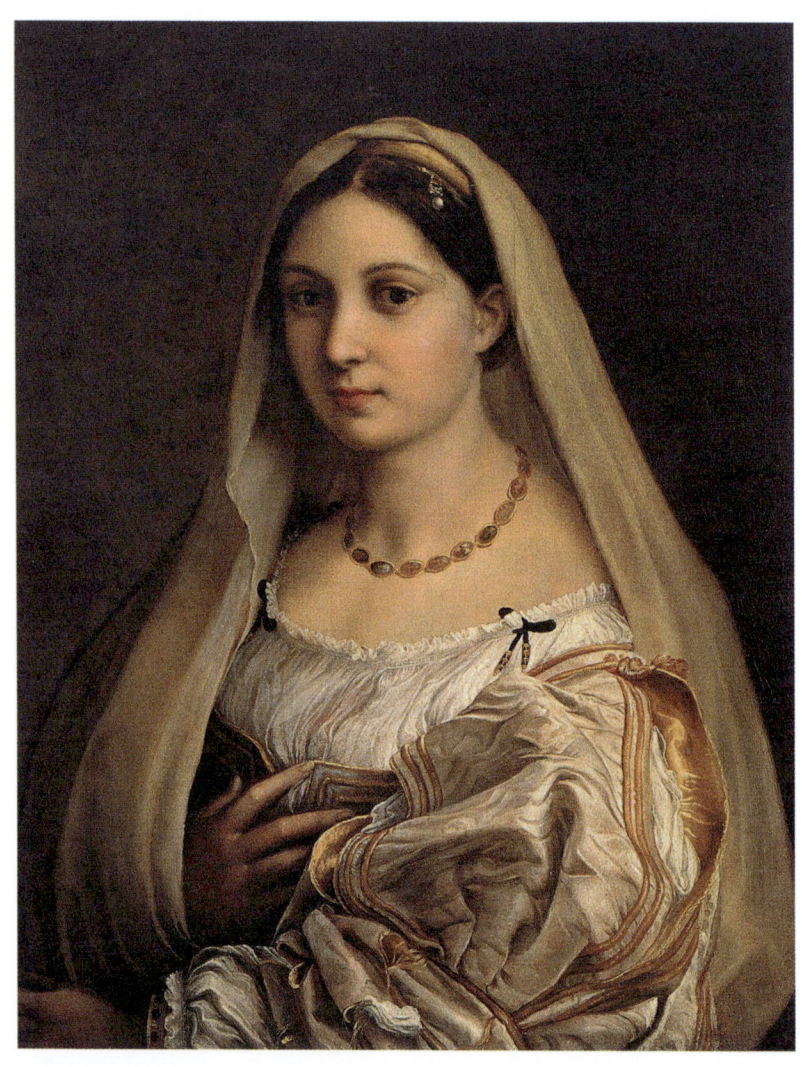

The Veiled Lady (La Donna Velata), Raphael, c.1513

Vasari identifies her as the woman in a portrait known as *The Veiled Lady* (*La Donna Velata*) dated to about 1513 or 1514.

Look at it alongside *The Portrait of a Young Woman* (*La Fornarina*). We can't tell much from the similarities in the hairline because the central parting was a common style, though the stray curls which have fallen across La Donna's temple add to a sense that this is a deeply personal portrait. But the eyes, and the shape of the ear and nose, surely suggest we are looking at the same woman. And – physical resemblance aside – there is that same slightest suggestion of a smile playing on La Donna's lips just as in La Fornarina's portrait. The main contrast is obvious – here the sitter is fully clothed. And if she was indeed a baker's daughter, then Raphael, who was a very rich man by this time, shows her in the finest of white and gold silks, with a fine pearl and ruby in her hair (slightly different from the one worn by La Fornarina) and with a meticulously detailed necklace of agates set in gold.

Raphael painted very few portraits of women (there is probably only one other) and these are the only two which evoke anything like the same degree of intimacy between artist and model. Do they represent the same person? It certainly seems so, and if they do then she is surely the woman who, as Vasari states, was the love of Raphael's life.[24]

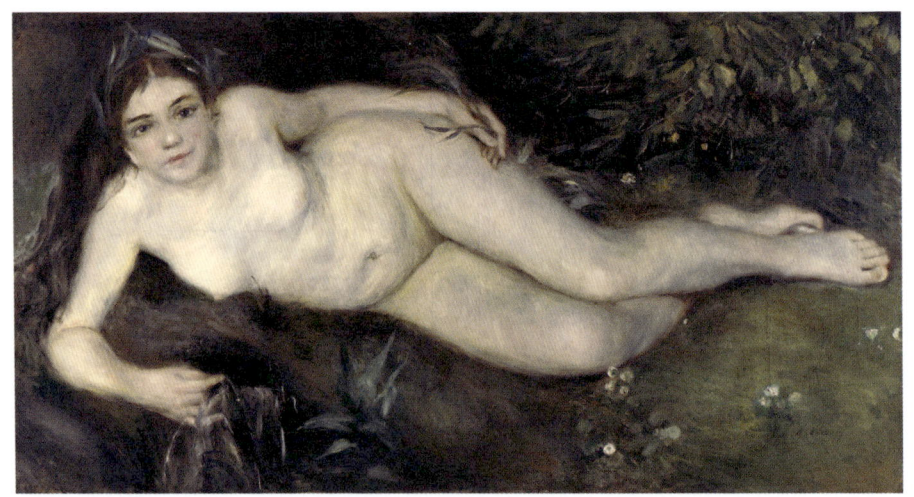

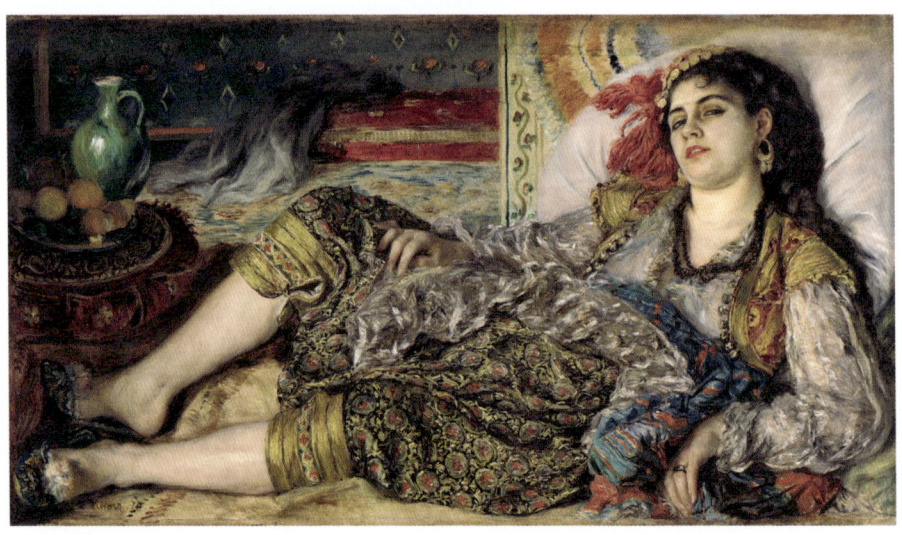

(Top) *A Nymph by a Stream*, Renoir, 1869–1870
(Above) *Odalisque (Woman of Algiers)*, Renoir, 1870

Impressions of Passion

Renoir & Lise Tréhot

This explicitly sensual painting, *A Nymph by a Stream*, was probably made in 1869 or 1870 and marks the first time that Lise Tréhot (1848–1922) agreed to pose naked for her lover, Pierre-Auguste Renoir (1841–1919). The pair had met in the spring of 1866. Renoir was 25 and beginning to find his way as an artist; Lise, the daughter of a tobacconist in Paris, had just turned 18. They seem to have been introduced by her older sister, Clémence, who was having an affair with Renoir's friend, the painter Jules Le Coeur. He would invite Renoir to his house and studio at Bourron-Marlotte on the edge of the Fontainebleau forest. Several of Renoir's earliest paintings of Lise show her as a demure figure in a flowing white dress against a background of fields or woods.

A Nymph by a Stream is a distinct departure from those rather small-scale, informal sketches. Almost life-sized, it is one of the first nudes made by Renoir, and it is also the first time that he pictured Lise looking out of the picture, making direct eye contact with her lover as he painted. Yet it also represents a curious mix of personal connection and artistic formality. While Renoir has clearly made Lise recognizable, he also casts her not as herself, but lying by a stream in the guise of a naiad – or water nymph – from the world of Greek mythology. This was

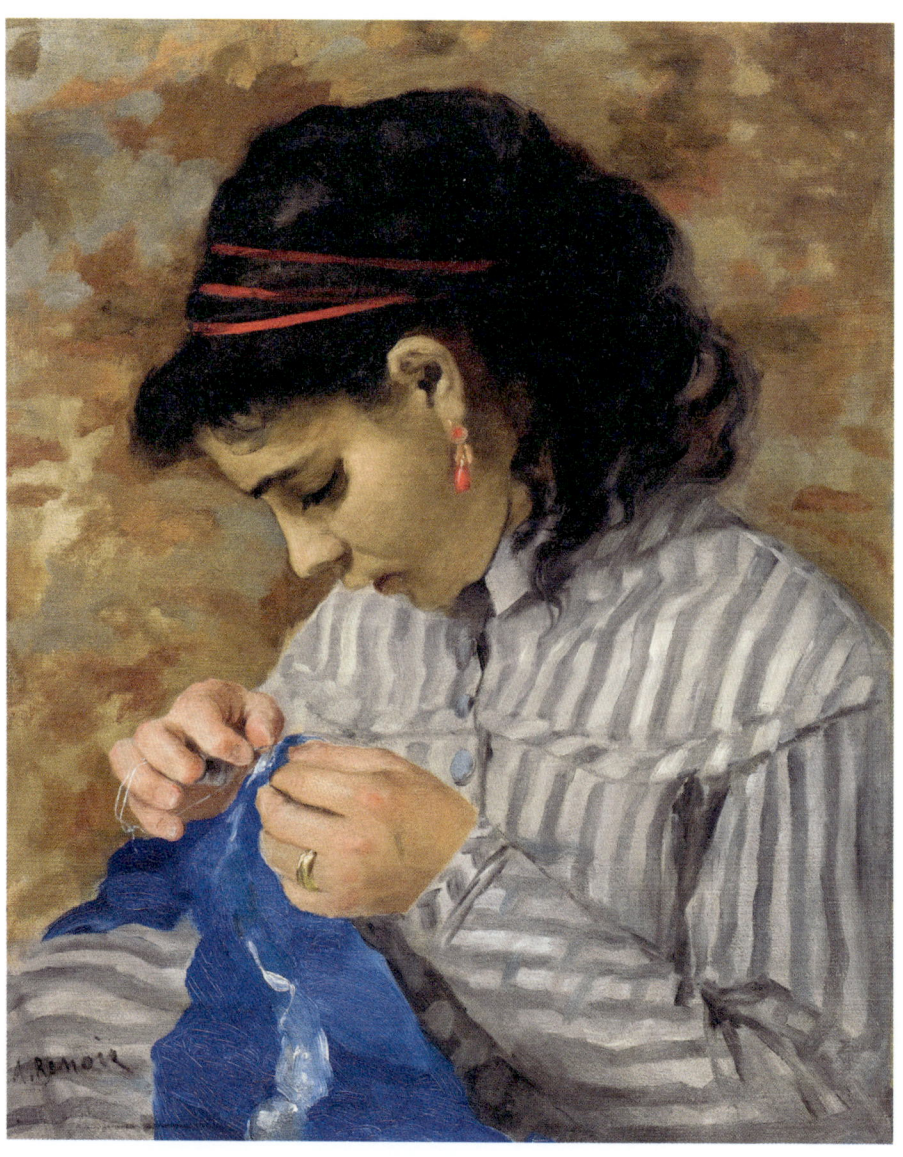

Lise Sewing, Renoir, c.1867

a popular theme among contemporary artists; a good excuse to paint an erotic female nude, rather than to explore a character or a relationship.

The image doesn't stand alone. It also needs to be considered alongside another picture he made around the same time. *Odalisque (Woman of Algiers)* is painted on the same-sized canvas and depicts Lise in a very similar pose – only reversed, a reflected image of the water nymph as it were. Here again, Lise is playing an erotic role, but instead of showing her naked, Renoir dresses her in an exotic oriental costume as though she were a concubine in a harem – another favourite theme in Paris artistic circles of the time, and one that was obviously loaded with sexual innuendo.

In some ways, *Odalisque (Woman of Algiers)* is the more explicit of the two paintings. Once again, Lise looks directly at the viewer, but this time the expression is less neutral. While the naked nymph looks slightly up at us with wide-eyed innocence, here Lise's parted lips are reddened, her half-closed eyes are heavily lined with black makeup and she looks down knowingly at the viewer.

When you hang the paintings together – which must have been Renoir's intent – other dynamics emerge. There is the obvious frisson of depicting the same woman twice – first clothed, then naked – and there is also a clear reference to a famous artistic precedent. Renoir must have known the two most celebrated paintings by the Spanish artist, Francisco Goya (1746–1828) – *The Naked Maja* and *The Clothed Maja* – which were also designed to be compared in this way.

Renoir painted Lise more than 20 times during their six-year affair and often there is a deep sense of his connection to her. *Lise Sewing*, made early on in their relationship (in 1866 or 1867), is an intensely personal study of a woman absorbed in her work. And *Woman in Repose, Half-Naked: the Rose*,[25] which may be the last painting Renoir made of his lover before they split in 1872, seems to hark back to those early sketches in Fontainebleau forest. It is on the same small scale, but it is set in the bedroom rather than the woods. The flowing white dress – perhaps it is a nightdress – has been half abandoned, and though Lise's attention seems distracted, wistful even, she holds the rose in an extremely suggestive position.

Within a year, however, the relationship was over. Lise became involved with an architect called Georges Brière de l'Isle whom she married a decade later in 1883. There are no accounts of exactly how the split with Renoir happened. We do know that Lise never saw Renoir again. Perhaps she began to resent her lack of status. Although his friends and Lise's own family knew about the relationship, and he even attached her first name to some of his portraits of her, Renoir never formally acknowledged her publicly as his lover. Nor did he acknowledge paternity when Lise gave birth to a daughter, Jeanne, in July 1870, though after Jeanne was given up for adoption, Renoir did make secret arrangements to support his daughter financially until his death in 1919 and met her on several occasions.

Perhaps Lise simply tired of Renoir and fell in love with Brière de l'Isle. If so, her memories of those years with him seem to have been powerful ones – she kept his painting of her sewing all her life. But the love letters and papers which would have told us so much more, she burned just before she died in 1922.[26]

Woman in Repose, Half-Naked: the Rose, Renoir, 1872

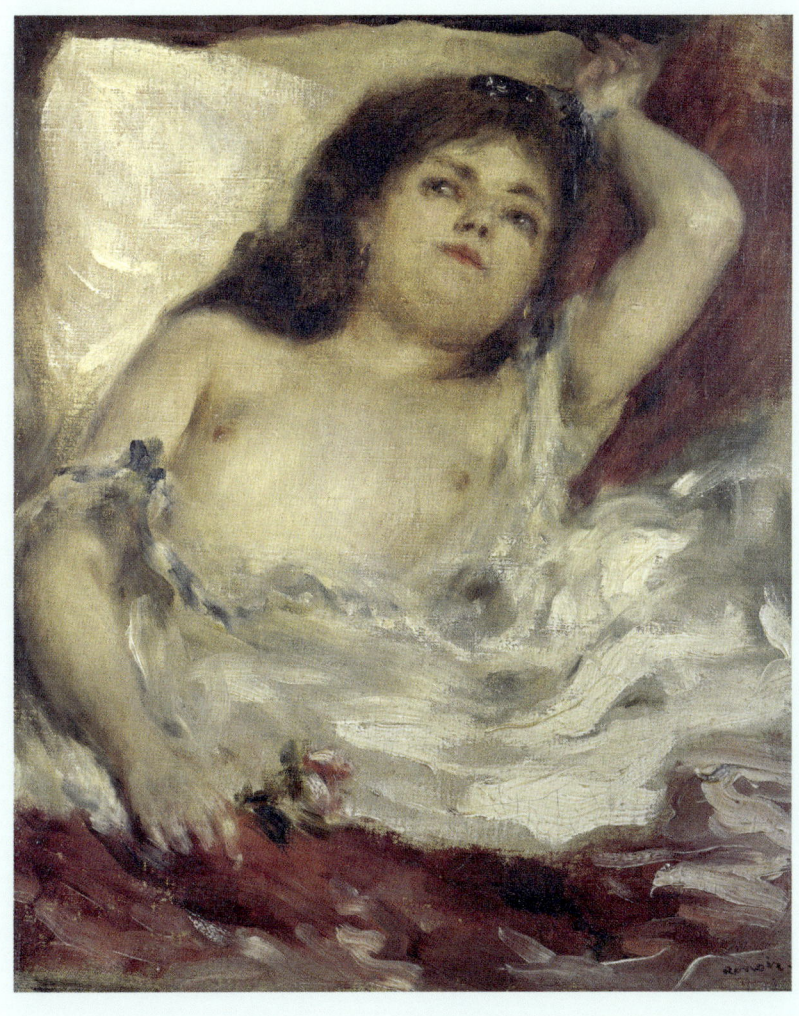

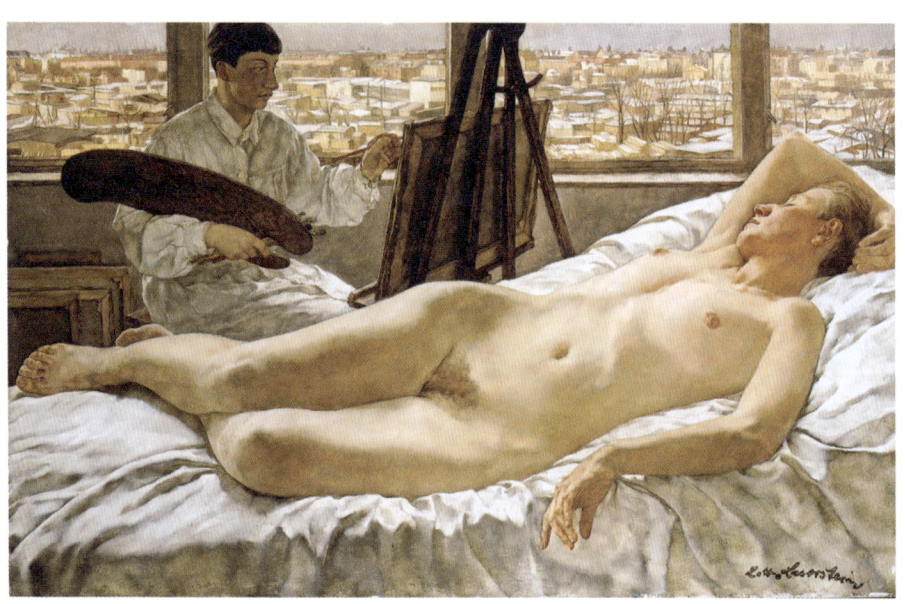

In My Studio, Lotte Laserstein, 1928

Naked Abandon

Lotte Laserstein & Traute Rose

*I*n *My Studio* is Lotte Laserstein's (1898–1993) characteristically understated title for this highly charged portrait of herself and her close friend Traute Rose (born Gertrud Süssenbach, 1903–1989), who lies naked on the bed before her.

The image works on several levels. Rose is depicted in a pose of dreamy abandon and there is a powerful tension between the reverie of the sleeping model and the intense focus of Laserstein who, cloaked in the shadows of the background, applies herself diligently to her painting.

There is a monumental side to the composition, too. Rose's body, bathed in light, takes up a quarter or more of the canvas. The palette of whites and flesh tones in the foreground reflects the colours of the snow-covered rooftops through the windows. The curves and undulations of Rose's torso laid out on the white sheet have become a landscape in their own right.

There is also a playful dimension. The painting positions us as voyeurs both of the naked Rose and of the artist herself, who does not meet our eye and who is also apparently unaware of our presence. However, we know that things are more complicated than this. Laserstein depicts herself intent on her easel but to compose the scene, she must be looking at a mirror and she implicitly signals this, by showing herself painting with her left hand, when she was actually right-handed. Finally, there is the question of what the painting tells us about the relationship between the two women. When it was made, in 1928, they were both living in Berlin. Laserstein had been one of the first women to study at the Academy of Fine Arts in Berlin and had set herself up in a studio as a portraitist. Rose had trained as a dance gymnast but was to become a photographer and later a painter. She sat as a model for Laserstein many times, for formal portraits, as a nude and also engaged in everyday activities such as washing herself.

This was extremely unusual for the time. Even by the late 1920s, in the liberal atmosphere of Weimar Berlin, it was considered a radical statement for a woman to paint a naked body from life. To do so in such a direct and explicit way was exceptionally bold; comparable with what the daring and provocative Tamara de Lempicka was doing in Paris (see p136).

But does it, as is so clear in some of Lempicka's work, suggest physical desire between the artist and model? There is no doubt that the two formed a close bond, but neither admitted to an affair. A strong clue as to the intimacy of their relationship, however, lies not only in this full-frontal nude, but in the tender and physical way the two women relate to each other in other double portraits which Laserstein painted around the same time. A series of sketches she made of Rose sleeping naked in bed also strongly suggest they were lovers.

However, both had relationships with men. Laserstein was engaged to the Hungarian painter Palo Vidor between 1920 and 1924, before she ended the relationship, apparently to focus on her artistic career.[27] And after an intense period in the later 1920s and early 1930s when most of the portraits by Laserstein were made, Traute went on to marry the writer Ernst Rose in 1933. Four years later, Laserstein, who was partly of Jewish ancestry, married a Swedish man in order to escape from Nazi Germany to Sweden. But they did not move in together and she lived independently until her death in 1993.

It was considered a radical statement for a woman to paint a naked body from life.

The Painter and Traute Rose, Lotte Laserstein, 1963

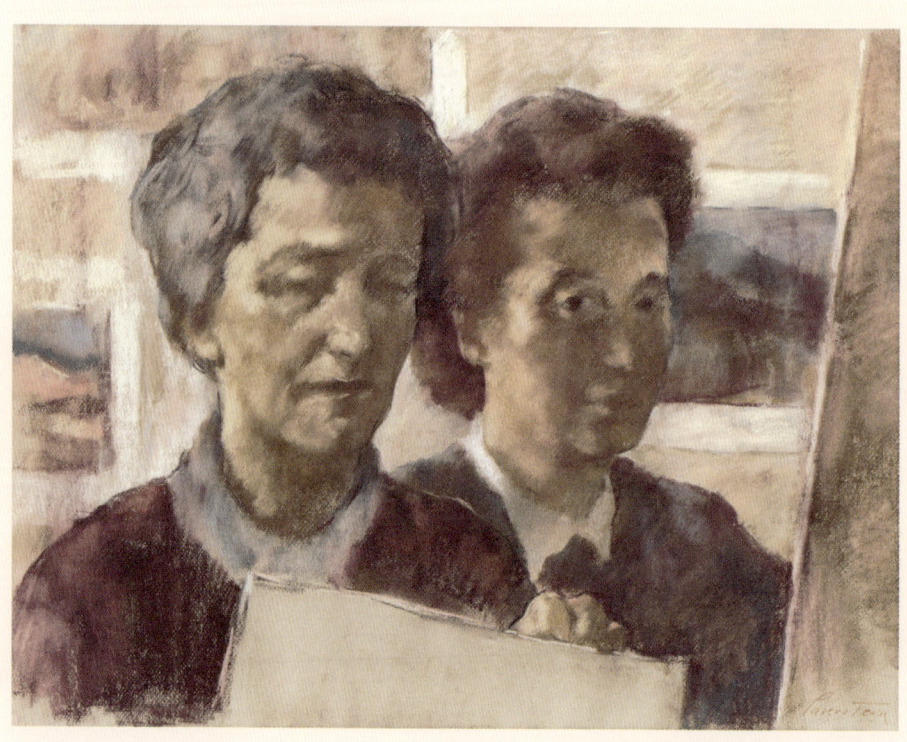

The deep friendship between the two women endured, however. They worked together for more than 50 years, with Traute and her husband visiting Laserstein at her Swedish summer home nearly every year once the war was over.[28] That sense of collaboration between artist and model is apparent in several of the many paintings made of Rose by Laserstein. The fact that the women considered them a combined effort is regularly hinted at in the artist's letters in which she refers to them as 'our' paintings. In a letter from Laserstein to Rose, written in 1971, many years after the 1920s portraits, she wrote, nostalgically: 'when I think of what we could accomplish then, the artist and the model'.[29]

The collaborative spirit is again made explicit in the double portrait of 1963 where both women are depicted in the act of creation. It is a self-portrait of Laserstein painting, with Rose in the foreground, drawing. There is a particular resonance here, not only because it evokes their shared creative mission, but because it echoes the composition of another early painting, *I and My Model,* which she had made in 1928, the same year as *In My Studio.*[30] She seems to be paying tribute to an intimacy and a bond that had endured for more than 35 years.

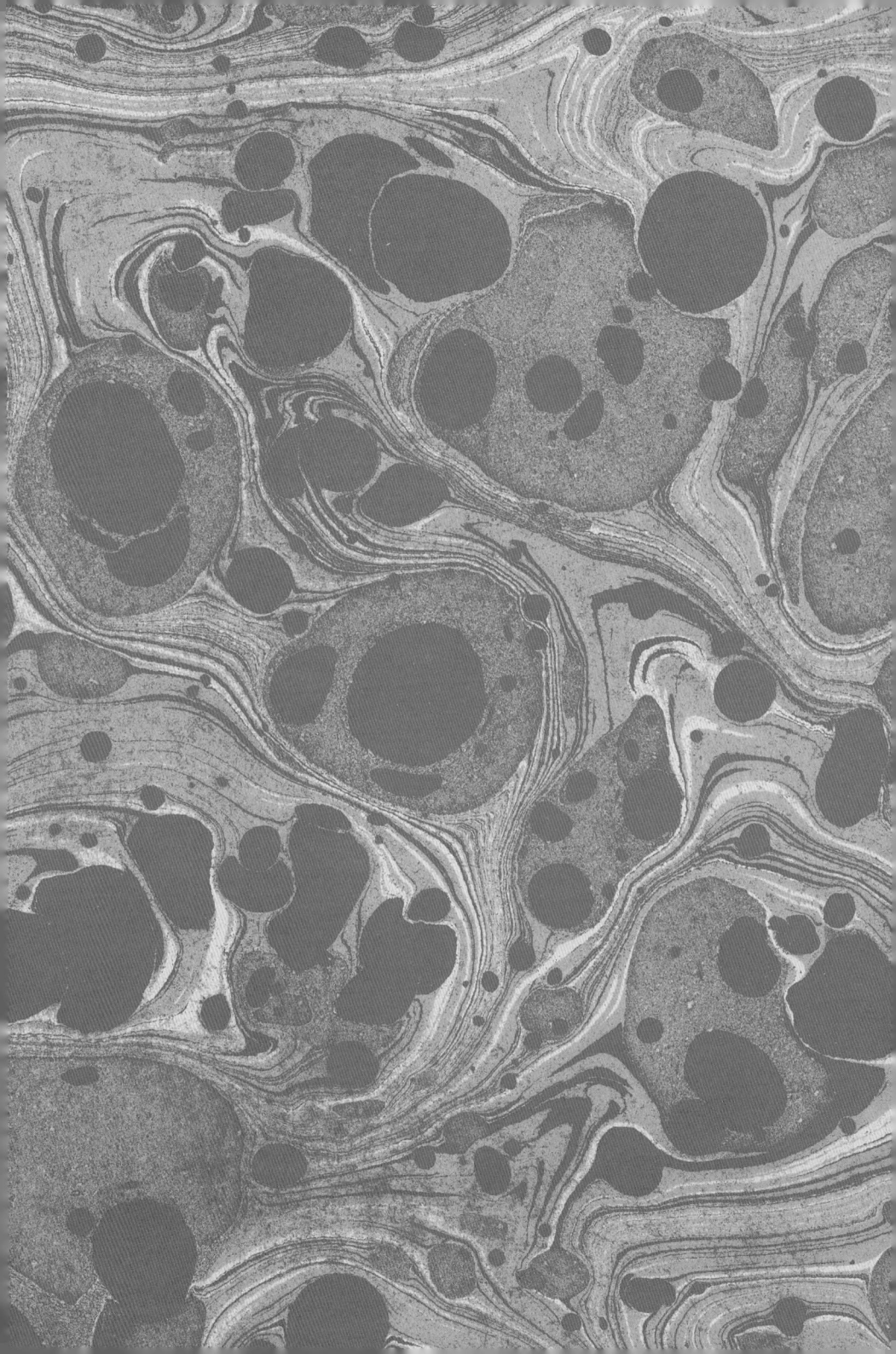

SERIAL

LOVERS

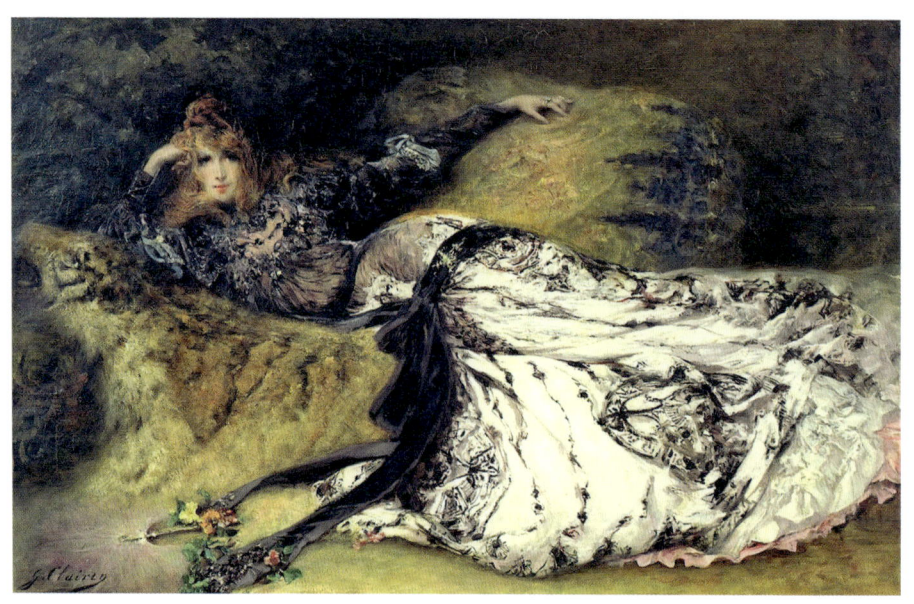

Portrait of Sarah Bernhardt, George Clairin, 1871

Love in the Spotlight

Sarah Bernhardt

It's the most sensual and luxurious of images. A young woman with untamed auburn hair and bright red lipstick stretches herself out voluptuously on a tiger skin. The artist revels in her sinuous form – elongating her left arm so it drifts languidly into the background. Her legs seem never-ending – her feet lost in her frothing skirts. In fact, there is something of the mermaid – or siren, as the French would say – about the way it fans out on to the rug. There is a suggestive tension, too, in the pink frills of her petticoats and the extravagant black velvet bow which is tied around her hips. Is this some sort of gift-wrapping?

She certainly seems to be advertising her availability, if only to the artist. Her dress has slipped so far down that her midriff is covered only by a chiffon negligee which forms a sort of gossamer frisson between her body and the warm, soft tiger fur. In his turn, the artist, Georges Clairin (1843–1919), is clearly delighting in that frisson and the fact that the model, Sarah Bernhardt (1844–1923), is entirely aware of the magnetic power she has over him.

The painting was made in the early 1870s when Bernhardt was about 27 and Clairin was a year older. He was a relatively minor painter during a time when Paris was the world centre of art – but Sarah Bernhardt was then probably the single most famous woman in the city. The daughter of a well-connected courtesan, she had already had a string of high-society lovers of her own and borne a son by a Belgian prince. Then, in her 20s, she had shot to fame as a charismatic actor with – as Clairin's portrait captures so effectively – an astonishingly powerful stage presence. As Victor Hugo said in 1872, 'She is adorable; she is better than beautiful, she has the harmonious movements and looks of irresistible seduction.' [31]

She also had a talent for making headlines so that everyone wanted to see her act, whether in new plays, comedies, tragedies or classic roles. She filled theatres, made her own fortune and was to go on to enjoy worldwide fame, touring Europe and the United States and acting in early silent films. She specialized in both male and female roles, playing, for example, both Lady Macbeth and Hamlet (she was also, in 1900, the first-ever actor to play Hamlet on film). But she also had other artistic talents. By the 1870s, she was becoming skilled in sculpture and in 1875 had already made a striking plaster bust of Clairin. It's a dashing depiction, which shows his head set back in the way of an artist in front of an easel.

Clairin was – as the intimacy of his portrait of her makes clear – her lover. Or, more accurately, one of her lovers. Her many affairs included liaisons with the future King Edward VII, Victor Hugo, the artist Gustav Doré and several of the leading men with whom she starred on the stage. In 1882, she married Aristides Damala, a handsome Greek diplomat with a terrible reputation as a womanizer, but it was not a stable relationship and it was effectively over after only a few months.

Rarely, if ever, was Bernhardt monogamous, but thanks to the bohemian freedoms afforded to the creative and wealthy in Belle Époque Paris, she was able to live life by her own rules. She had lifelong relationships both with Clairin and another artist, Louise Abbéma. In 1875, the two women had commemorated their bond by making moulds of their hands clasped together in an eternal grasp and having them cast in bronze. Abbéma

Cast of the clasped hands of Sarah Bernhardt and Louise Abbéma, 1875

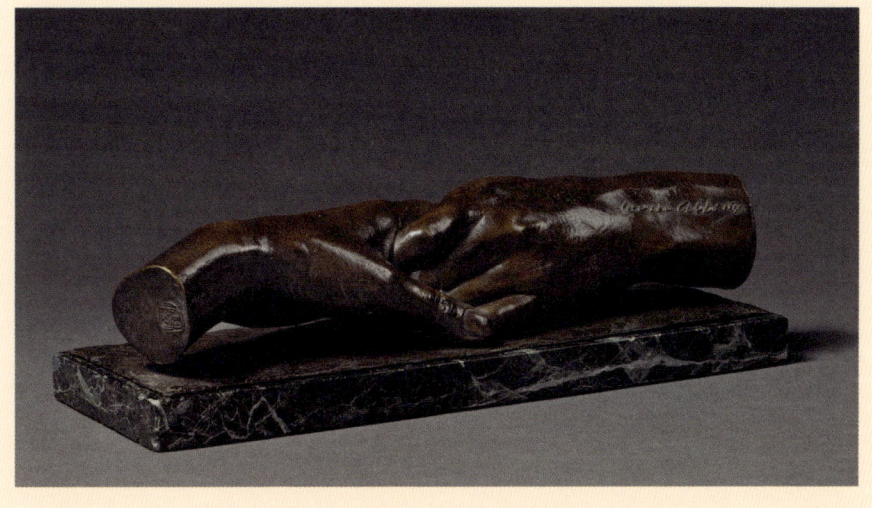

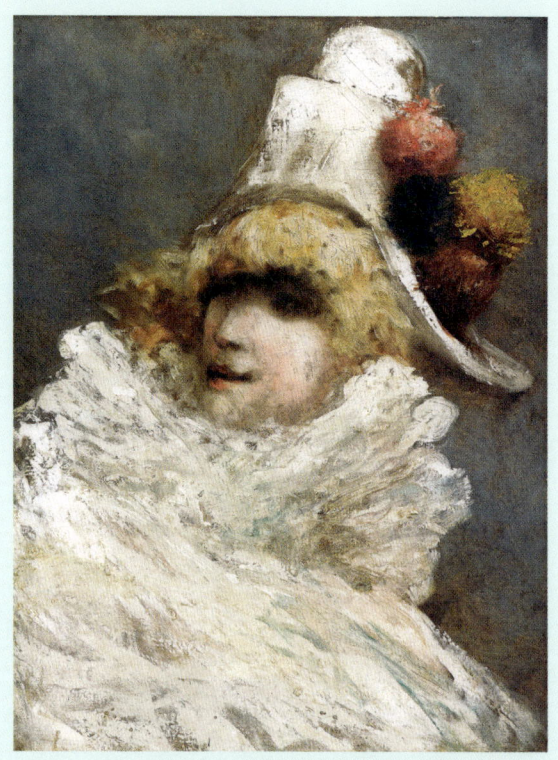

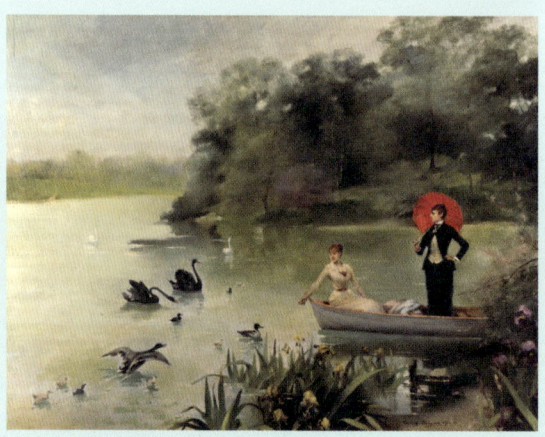

(Top) *Self-Portrait as Pierrot*, Sarah Bernhardt, c.1910
(Above) *Sarah Bernhardt and Louise Abbéma on a Lake*, Louise Abbéma, 1883

also made many paintings of Bernhardt, several of which show them together as a couple. One of the most striking dates from 1883 and depicts them in a rowing boat on the lake at the Bois de Boulogne. It plays heavily with contemporary perceptions of gender. Abbéma casts herself as a genteel lady, sitting demurely in the bow feeding the ducks. Bernhardt is dressed in masculine style, with a formal black jacket and long skirt, which, at first glance, might pass for trousers. Her profile is distinctly feminine however, the waistcoat buttoned tightly to emphasize her waist and the jacket cut to shape over her hips. She stands in protective, patriarchal fashion, watching over her friend and lover.

By contrast, one of Bernhardt's most fascinating paintings is a late self-portrait, in which she depicts herself in an entirely different guise. She is dressed as Pierrot, the hapless clown from the comic pantomime tradition, who was always sad and vulnerable, often with a black tear painted on his white face. He was normally portrayed for laughs, as a victim of unrequited love for a woman called Columbine. But in the 1880s, Bernhardt played him with a much darker side in a new play, *Pierrot Assassin*, in which he is persuaded by Columbine to commit murder for money. He is eventually arrested and blames his fate on her. So, in many ways, it is a sobering image. But it also memorializes another chapter in her love life: she, of course, had had an affair with the play's author, Jean Richepin.

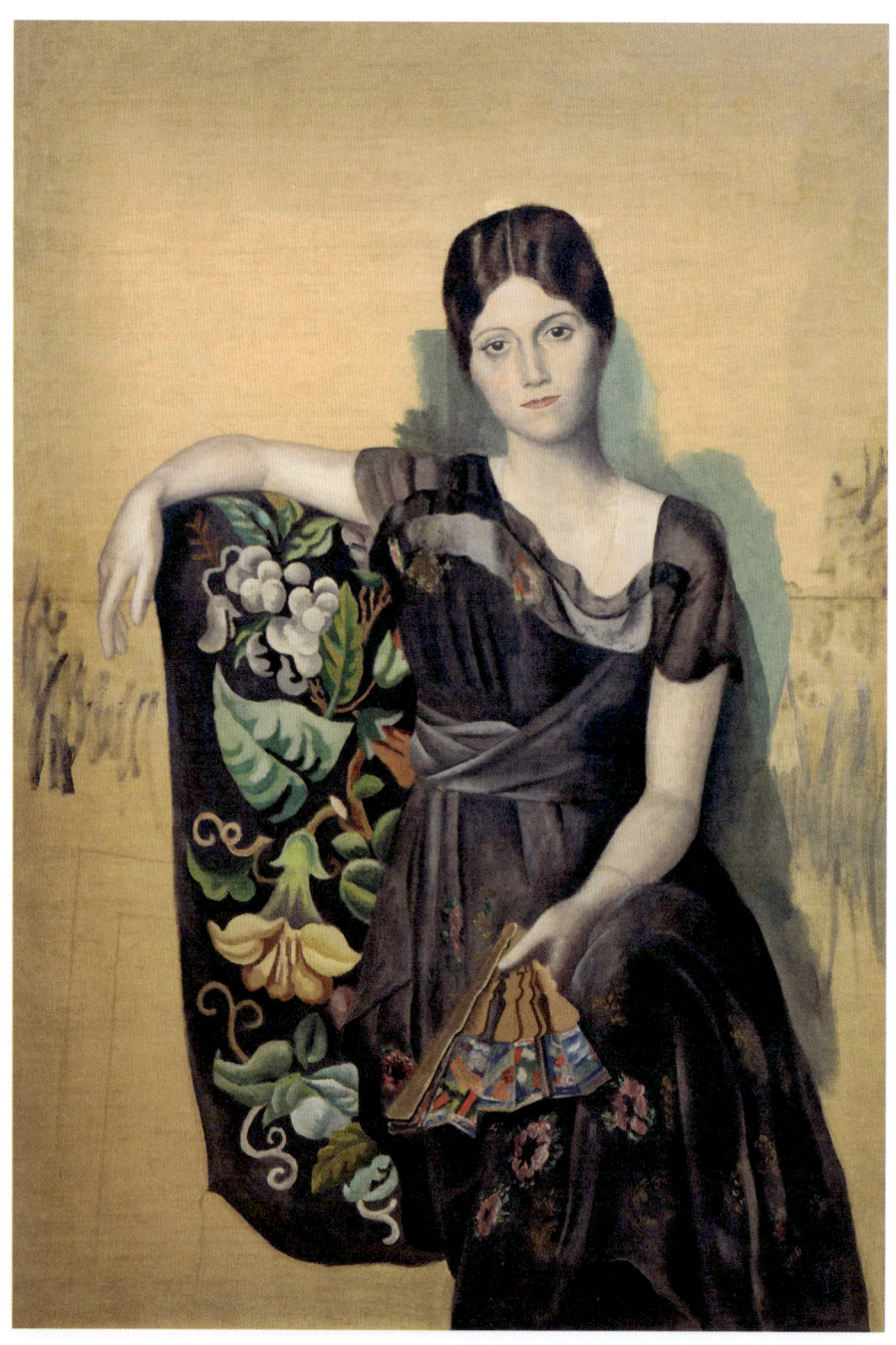

Portrait of Olga in an Armchair, Pablo Picasso, 1918

Tainted Love

Picasso, Olga & Marie-Thérèse

Olga Khokhlova was in Picasso's headlights from the moment they met in Rome in 1917. 'My dear, I have just received your letter with the 17 "I love yous". I counted them immediately and I am very happy. It's my favourite number,' she wrote in reply to one of his adoring letters.[32] She was a 26-year-old Russo-Ukrainian ballet dancer, working with the Ballets Russe. He was 36, a famous and controversial artist who had just designed the set for one of the ballet's most famous productions, *Parade*. And, as was his wont with his lovers, Picasso began painting her soon after they met. This portrait seems to have been made to mark the couple's engagement in 1918 and presents her as a poised and respectable fiancée. Though they were in Paris, she is wearing a Spanish-style dress which he had bought for her when he took her to visit his mother in Barcelona and she holds that essential Spanish accessory – a fan.

We can sense the adoration behind the painting. Olga is calm, composed and sitting slightly sideways on a chair brightly upholstered with flowers, which seems to float in indeterminate space. Picasso has left the background unfinished deliberately, as though all that mattered in the picture was Olga and her floral throne. But there is diffidence in the way she perches on one side of the chair and a sadness to her expression, her eyes cast down in inward reflection. Admittedly, in few portraits do Picasso's lovers look him in the eye – it is almost as though his gaze is too fierce to meet. But Olga's sadness perhaps stems more from her own wider anxieties. She was often ill during this year and her family, trapped in Russia, was caught in the throes of war and revolution.

Perhaps, too, there is a slightly detached, impersonal feel to the portrait. The colours are a little cold, Olga's skin somewhat greyish. One reason for this may be that it is one of the first examples of Picasso using black-and-white photography as part of his compositional technique. He worked partly from a photograph of Olga in exactly this position, on the same chair.

We need to look at the painting in a wider perspective, too. In marrying Olga, Picasso seems to have been creating a new identity for himself. He was moving up the social scale, breaking away from the impoverished bohemia of the run-down artist studios in Montmartre where he had lived for nearly 20 years. Now rich and successful and with a beautiful, glamorous wife, he was part of a grander, much more prosperous milieu. The First World War was ending, the couple were to move into a fine apartment with a butler, cook, maid and chauffeur. The Picassos were becoming part of the Paris glitterati and spending their summers in Brittany and Normandy and, later, on the Côte d'Azur.

The picture is as much a record of that transformation as a declaration of love. More than that, it is also about Picasso the artist and his place in the pantheon of great painters. Olga's pose and poise and the fan she is holding are clear references to the portraits of women by his great Spanish predecessors, Velázquez and Goya, and to the French 19th-century painter, Ingres. With this painting, Picasso was very deliberately positioning himself squarely in that grand lineage.

If this self-conscious grandeur defuses the passion of the painting, things change in 1921 when Olga gives birth to their son Paul. A new warmth floods Picasso's work. Over the next two years he paints at least a dozen images of a mother with her young baby. The figures are statuesque, even monumental and perhaps not quite portraits. They are clearly inspired by Olga and Paul, however. They

Large Nude in a Red Armchair (Grand Nu au Fauteuil Rouge), Pablo Picasso, 1929

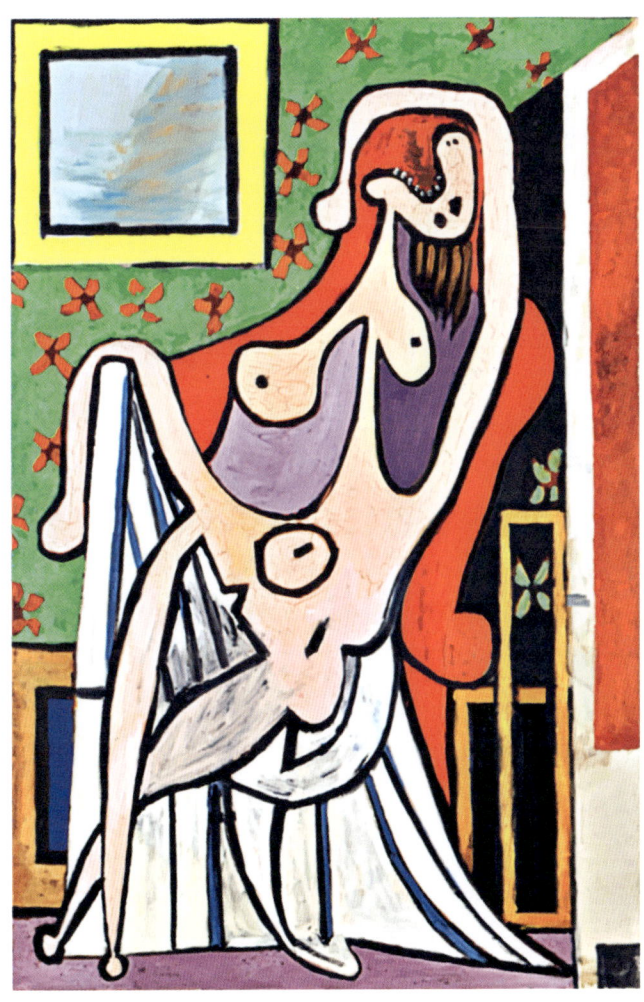

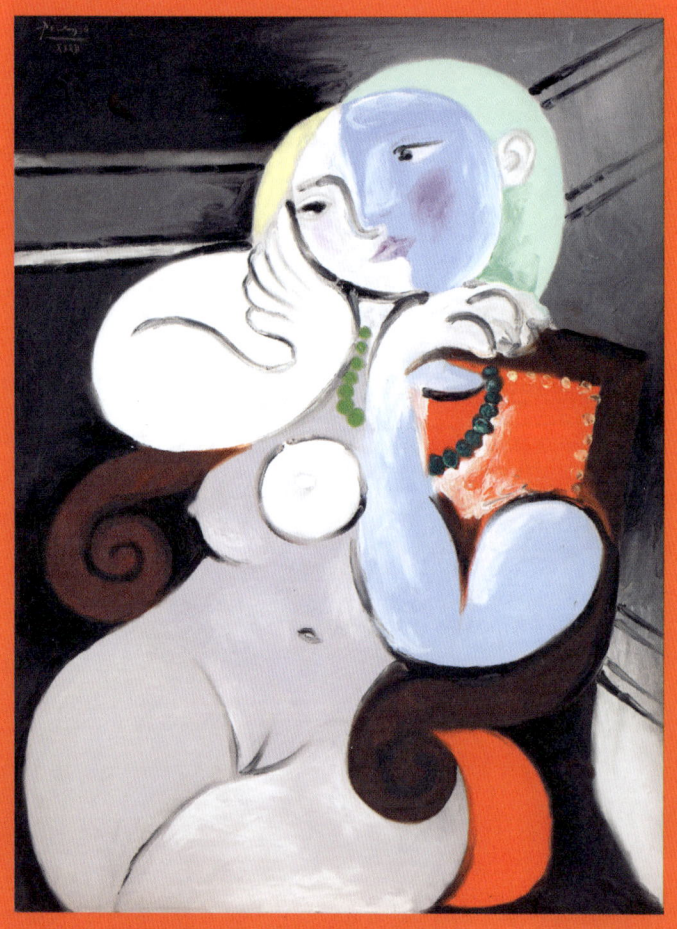

Nude Woman in a Red Armchair
(Femme Nue dans un Fauteuil Rouge), Pablo Picasso, 1932

conjure up both the art of the classical past and the long tradition of the Madonna with the young Christ and they also inhabit a quiet, parallel world of simplicity and tenderness, a happy time with his young family.

Then, within a few short years, it all goes wrong. Part of Picasso's creativity stemmed from his restlessness and his willingness to reject one lover brutally in favour of the next. He thrived on change, on conflict even. This is clear in his art, but it is also obvious from the way he treated a long succession of women. During the 1920s, he clearly tired of domestic imperatives and the demands of his wife and young child. In January 1927, the chance sighting of a beautiful 17-year-old girl in a Paris street proved too tempting for the frustrated 45-year-old artist. 'I am Picasso,' he tells Marie Thérèse Walter, 'I feel we are going to do great things together.' [33] And they do – in secret.

While he paints and sculpts his new lover with obsessive tenderness and care, developing a whole new artistic language of eroticism, Picasso also uses his art to destroy his desire for Olga. In his fierce creative crucible, she metamorphosizes from loving young wife and mother to a devouring monster. It's a merciless transformation. Compare the portrait Picasso made in 1929 – *Grand Nu au Fauteuil Rouge* – with the one of Olga in the Spanish dress from 11 years earlier. Those gentle hands have become lumpen fists; those soulful eyes, nothing but black holes. Her mouth is now a gaping jaw. Her elegant dress has been stripped from her and her body parts reduced to daubs and slits, the pink paint coagulated, the black outlines heavy and roughly made. No longer a throne, the chair seems instead like a macabre prop for her distorted form.

Compare this artistic evisceration to the portrait of Marie Thérèse (opposite) that he made three years later, as their relationship reached its erotic peak. She graces the sinuous lines of this red armchair with voluptuous curves. The colours are gentle and seductive; black moderates into grey, blue blends to white. The touch of the brush is so soft that outlines die away. Picasso is swooning with desire once more and we can see it in his art.

109

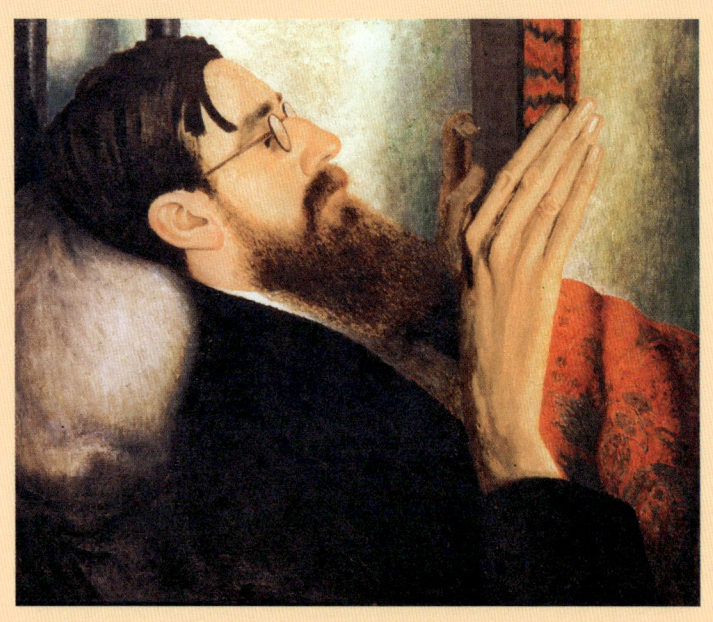

Lytton Strachey, Dora Carrington, 1916

Frustration & Fulfilment

Dora Carrington

'The world is rather tiresome ... ladies in love with buggers, and buggers in love with womanisers, and the price of coal going up too. Where will it all end'? [34]

That was the Bloomsbury Group writer, Lytton Strachey's (1880–1932) wittily dry assessment of his own love life in the summer of 1919. He was the homosexual, the lady was the artist, Dora Carrington (1893–1932) and the womanizer was a young publisher called Ralph Partridge (1894–1960) who was then on a cycling holiday in Cornwall with Carrington (as she was always known). It was a complicated situation which was eventually resolved by the establishment of a *ménage à trois*. Carrington married Partridge in 1921 and all three lived together for several years during the 1920s.

Carrington made this portrait of Strachey in 1916, before Partridge appeared on the scene. Strachey reclines on a sofa, his long red beard merging into the blanket that covers him. Seen in profile like this, holding up the book uncomfortably close to his face with his extraordinarily long angular hands, it is faintly reminiscent of a church funerary monument, of a medieval knight lying on his back in prayer. But it is not a cold portrait. Although the composition is full of strong diagonals and uprights, and captures a sense of awkwardness and detachment, the tight framing includes us in the space and makes us feel closer to Lytton. The palette is rich and warm, and the fabrics of the blanket, pillow and jacket soften the hard edges, while the hand is so finely and tenderly observed.

It's a suitable tribute to an enduring relationship in which sex sometimes got in the way of love. An anecdote from 1918 by Virginia Woolf is telling: 'After tea Lytton and Carrington left the room ostensibly to copulate; but suspicion was aroused by a measured sound proceeding from the room, and on listening at the keyhole it was discovered that they were reading aloud Macaulay's Essays!' [35]

That was the summer that Carrington met Partridge, whom Strachey also adored. The two men may have had a brief affair, but a relationship also developed between Dora and Ralph and led to their marriage in May 1921. None of several portraits she painted of him survive.

It was a marriage made not in heaven, but in the bohemian world of Bloomsbury. 'He knows I'm not in love with him',[36] Dora wrote to Lytton in 1921, a week before the wedding, and Ralph himself began having affairs almost straight away. However, she was in love with one of Partridge's best friends, the writer, Gerald Brenan (1894–1987), who lived in Spain and whom she, Ralph and Lytton had visited in 1920. He joined them all on a Lake District holiday in August 1921 and canoodled with Dora in secret while Ralph went fishing. The portrait she painted of him then could hardly be more different than the oblique view of Strachey. He gazes intently at the viewer with a smoulder of passion in his dark eyes. When he left to go home, she told him of her misery: 'my heart was almost breaking and my eyes crying'.[37]

By 1924, things were getting even more complicated. Carrington fell madly in love with a beautiful young American, Henrietta Bingham (1901–1968). Charismatic, wealthy, bisexual and extremely promiscuous, Bingham toyed with Carrington's affections and dropped her at the end of the year. But she had

Gerald Brenan, Dora Carrington, 1921

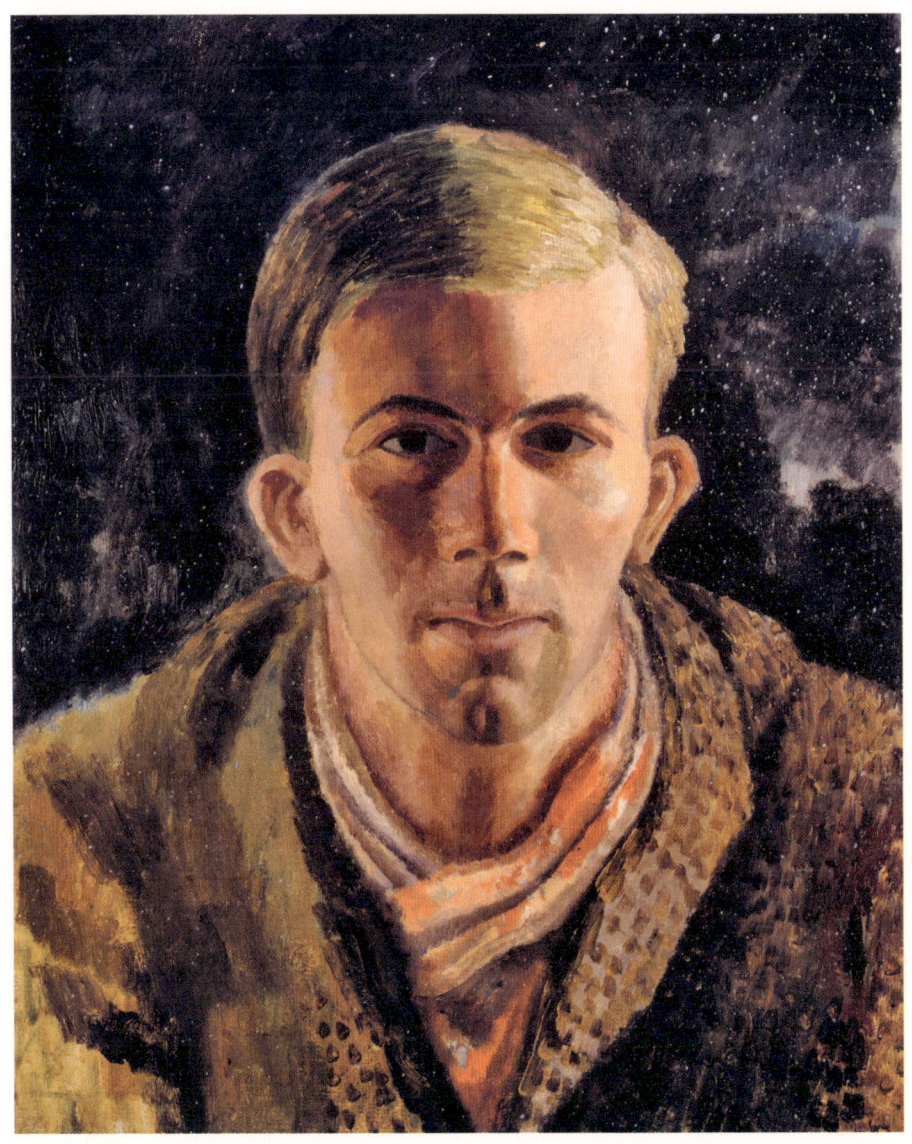

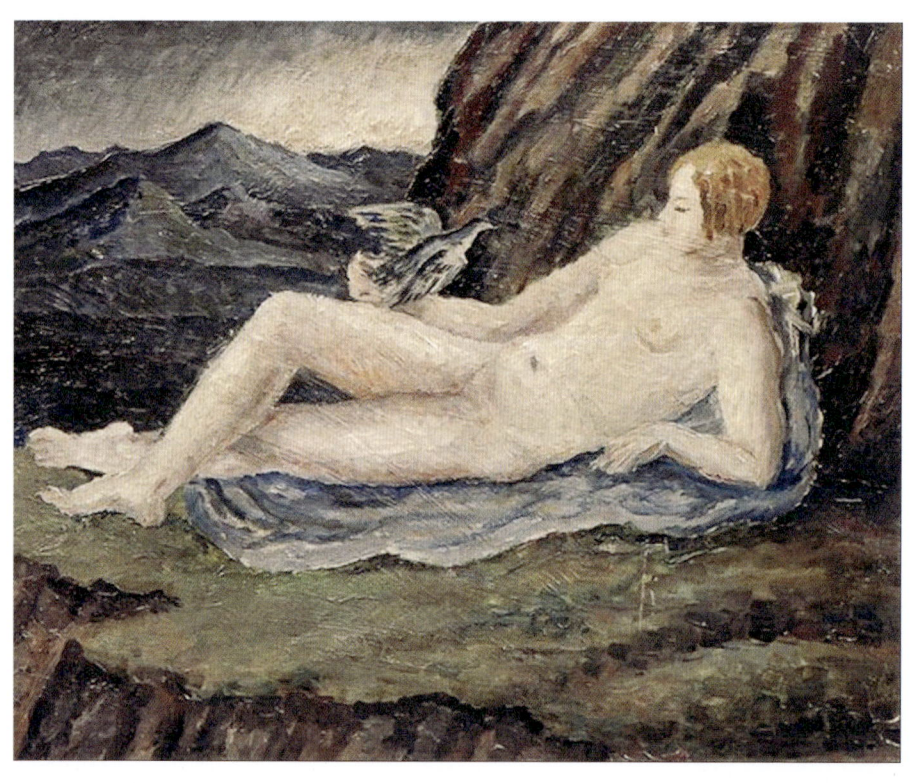

Reclining Nude with a Dove, Dora Carrington

ignited a new passion in her. 'I am very much more taken with H. than I have been with anyone for a long time. I feel now regrets at being such a blasted fool in the past, to stifle so many lusts I had in my youth, for various females',[38] she wrote during the affair, and remembering it later added: 'last summer with H [Henrietta]. Really I had more ecstacy [sic] with her, & no feelings of shame afterwards'.[39]

During the few brief months when Carrington was in love with Bingham, she made a portrait of her nude, reclining casually against a mountainous backdrop. The dove which has alighted on her hand is traditionally associated with Aphrodite, the goddess of love. It's really not much more than a sketch, but the easy physical confidence of Bingham is clear. The context is curious, however. She is placed on a ledge, and the imagery of the edge of the cliff in front of her is clearly suggestive. It hints at the physical sensations that she stirred in Carrington, but also emphasizes a sense of the unobtainable.

Carrington had several other affairs, but remained deeply attached to Strachey. The day before he died of stomach cancer in January 1932, she heard him whisper, 'Darling Carrington. I love her. I always wanted to marry Carrington and I never did.' She was deeply consoled: 'it was happiness to know he secretly had loved me so much'.[40] But she couldn't live with the loss. In February she wrote in her diary: 'I write in an empty book. I cry in an empty room. And there can never be any comfort again'.[41] In March she committed suicide with a borrowed shotgun.

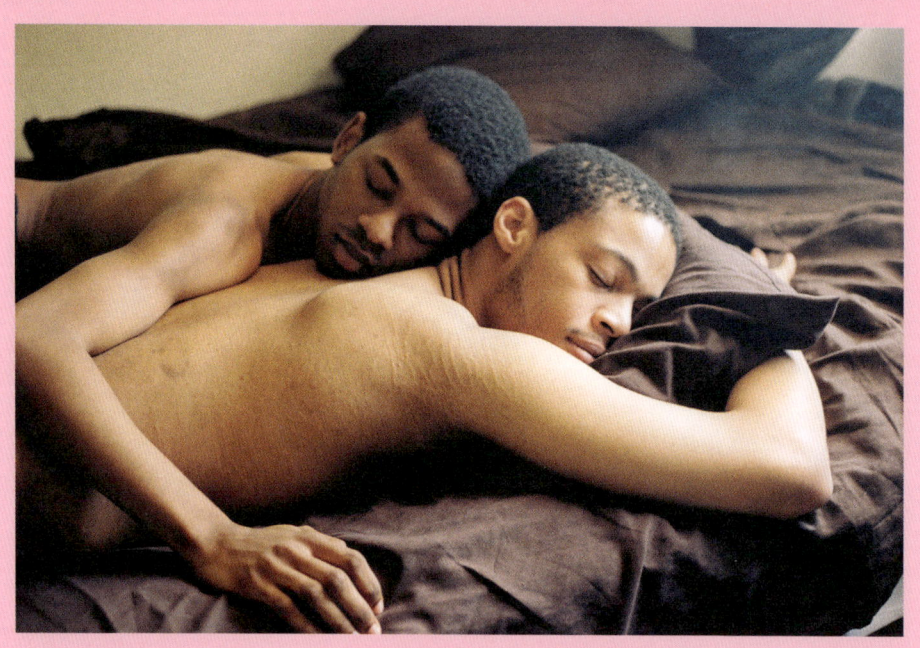

Sonny and David, Clifford Prince King, 2019

Love Through a Lens

Clifford Prince King

Two young men lie sleeping in an easy, contented embrace. It's the simplest of images, but *Sonny and David* (2019) is also an artful composition. The mirroring of the poses, the subtle graduation of tones and textures created by the colour of their skin, their short black hair, the deep shadows and the brown bed sheets – they all add to the sense of harmony. Youth and beauty are at peace and the men are content in their togetherness.

The creation of a sense that such an embrace was completely natural was at the forefront of the artist's mind. Clifford Prince King (b.1993), a young photographer who was born in Tucson, Arizona, and now lives in California, explained in an interview in 2021 that he wanted to create images he would like to have been exposed to while he was growing up. 'When I was younger I did not see images of Black queer men, particularly not in this soft light or in these tender moments'.[42]

He argues that most of the visual references that feature Black males have either come from 'traumatic films with hyper-masculine characters in them or are pretty sad'.[43] And when it comes to gay Black men that one dimensional characterization combines with an almost total absence of any kind of romantic imagery. They are simply not depicted in the same positive way as straight couples. 'We need more nuanced, positive and inspiring portrayals of blackness,' he says.[44]

That mission defines the way that King has created his images. His principal subjects are his friends and partners, and

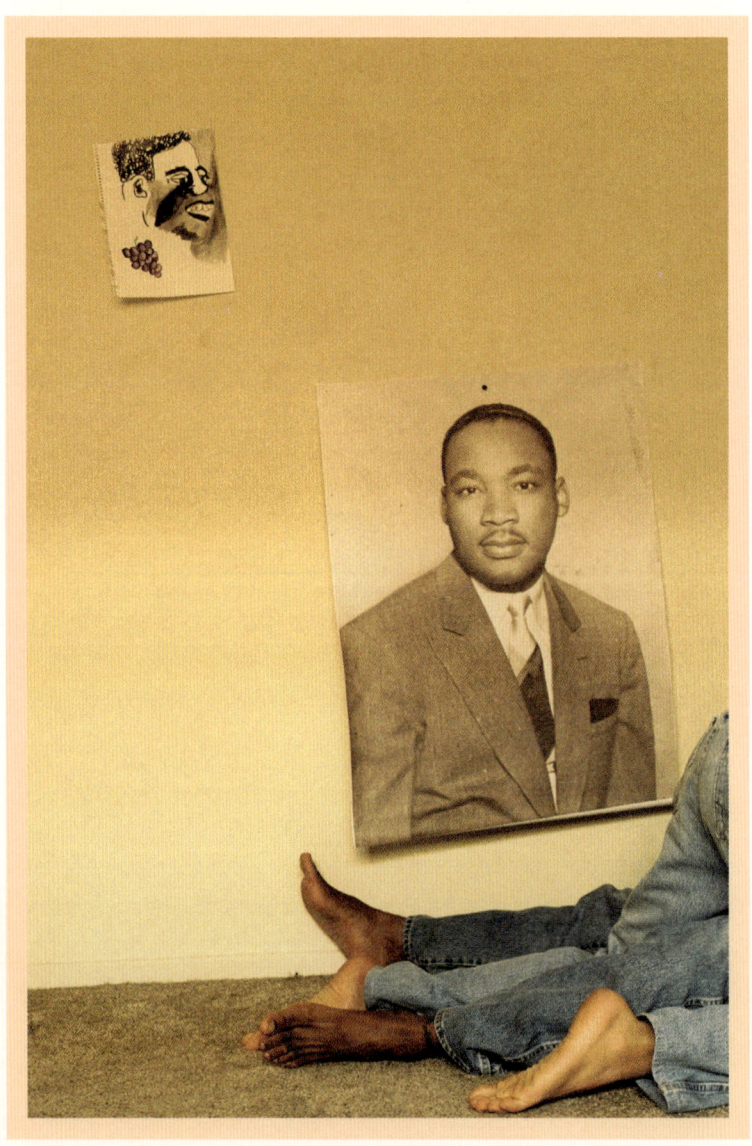

Poster Boys, Clifford Prince King, 2019

he depicts them in ordinary, domestic environments – kissing, holding hands, embracing. What we don't find in his work is a psychological study of an individual lover. In fact, he has explicitly said that he doesn't see his work as portraiture.[45] It is more concerned with those everyday intimacies of love and affection.

Being both Black and gay creates other dimensions to his portrayals of loving relationships. *Poster Boys* (2019) – a more cryptic image – depicts only the lower half of two men's bodies. It could be viewed as a sort of preamble to *Sonny and David*, another side to the physical story of two men sleeping together. They are still at least partially clothed, sprawled out on the carpet and clearly entwined in what seems to be a kiss or embrace, but which is hidden from our eyes. The light is not quite as golden, but it is still warm in tone – the slight shadow on the wall suggests perhaps that the blind has been half pulled down on a sunny day. A drawing torn from a sketch pad and taped to the wall depicts a man's face with a bunch of grapes – it adds a contemporary, light-hearted, Bacchic feel to the atmosphere.

But there is also a more political agenda to the composition which is alluded to in the title. According to King, the photograph of the young, earnest Martin Luther King Jr pinned so prominently to the wall in the background carries important meanings for the context and possibilities of love and relationships between gay people in his community. 'There is a lot of anti-gayness within the Black community and so I thought that having those references on the walls could bring these two worlds together,' he said when commenting on the image.[46] Martin Luther King Jr is an obvious symbol of a key moment in the battle for Black liberation a generation ago, but for Clifford Prince King there is another dimension to that liberation. Again referring to this photograph, he points out that, in his experience, the same people that are fighting for their rights in the way that Martin Luther King Jr did, can still be the ones he falls out with when discussing sexual liberation and preferences.[47]

By contrast, in *Orange Peel and Biktarvy* (2018) Clifford Prince King introduced a third dimension to the potential complexities, psychology and restraints which shadow the gay community. It is a simple still life, composed in tones of beige and orange which depicts the two halves of the fruit hollowed out – or perhaps, sucked dry – on a leather sofa next to two pills.

As the title makes clear, these are Biktarvy pills, an antiretroviral medication for the treatment of HIV/AIDS which had been licensed in the United States earlier that year and are a reference to King's own HIV diagnosis in 2018.

Five years later, he spoke again about the condition, saying that he managed his HIV by taking a single pill each day. He wanted to be hopeful about the situation and transmit that sense of hope to others with the same condition: 'Whether through my photography or simply with my everyday activism, I want to show people that there can also be a healthy, loving and successful side to the life of those living with HIV.' [48]

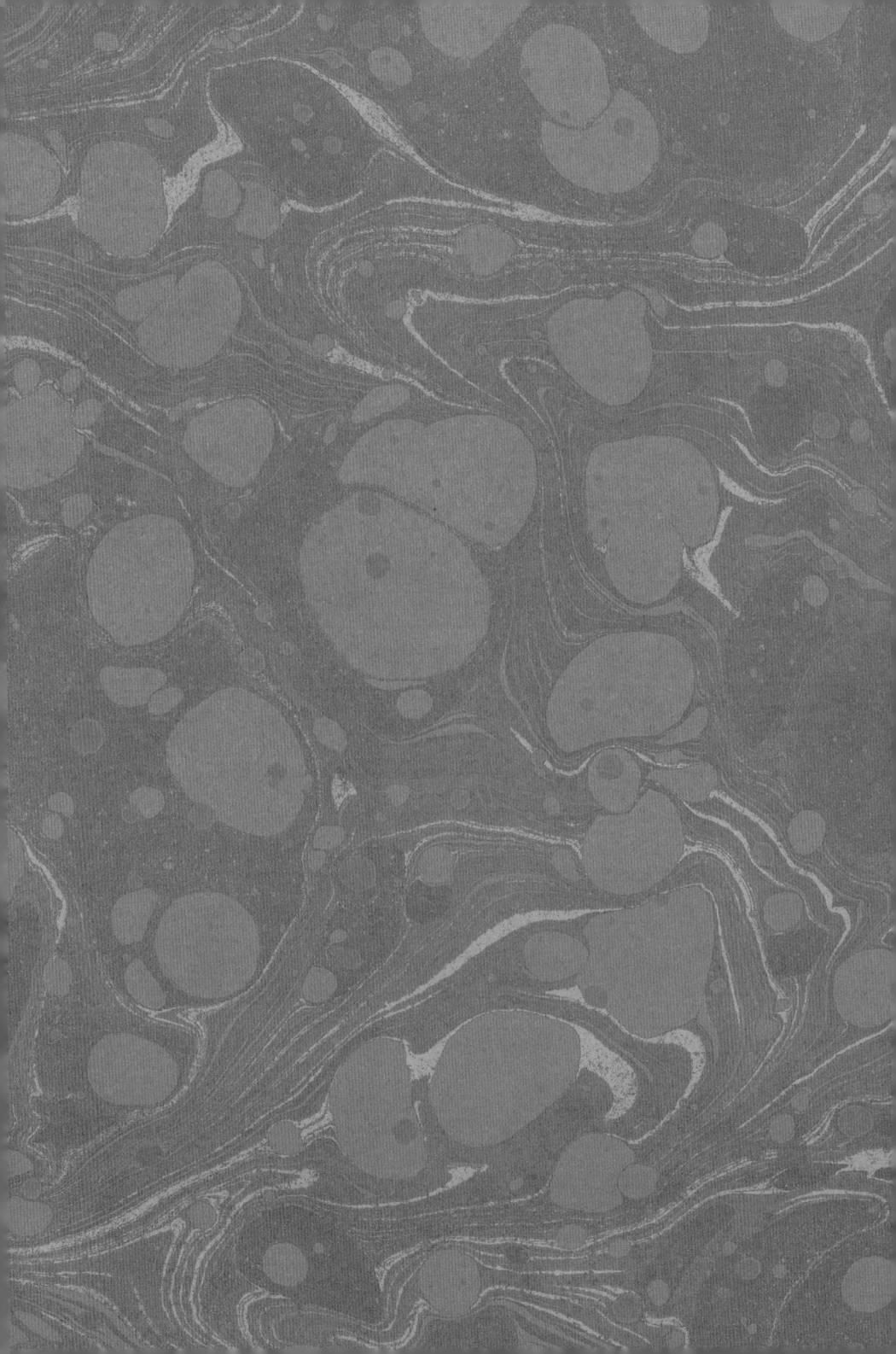

BURNING

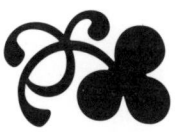

PASSIONS

Adam and Eve, Suzanne Valadon, 1909

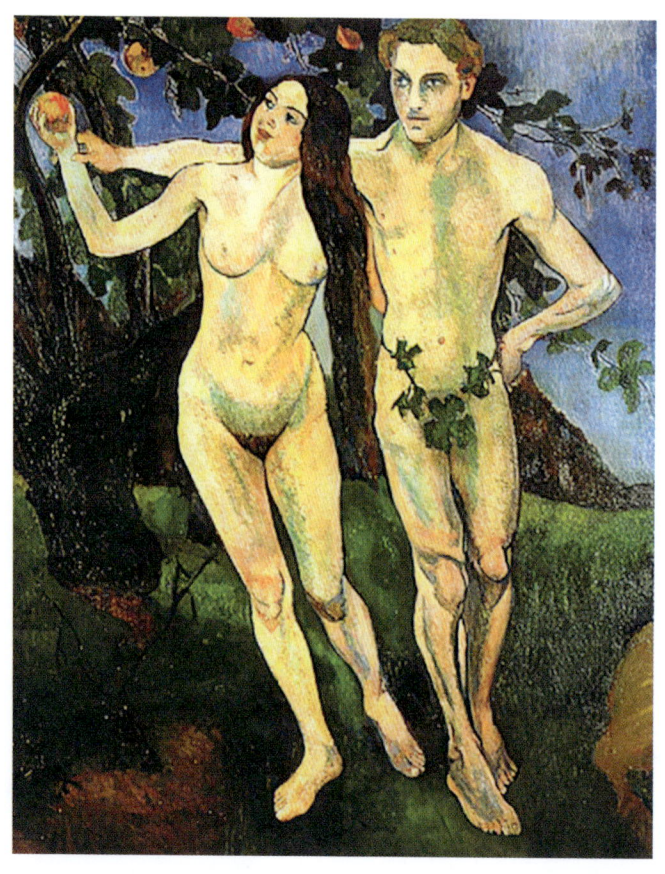

Forbidden Fruit

Suzanne Valadon & André Utter

A dam and Eve: this is an image loaded with contradictory meanings – ideas of betrayal, shame and rejection, but also of loyalty and devotion. They are the original loving couple, created for each other to live in perpetual bliss. But they are also doomed. When Eve eats the forbidden fruit from the tree of knowledge, so does Adam. Their innocence is lost and God casts them out of the Garden of Eden.

It was a favourite subject in the history of Western painting. But this near life-sized depiction by the artist Suzanne Valadon (1865–1938) takes the tradition a step further. She casts herself and her lover – the painter, André Utter – in the roles of the protagonists, and she has chosen to show the moment just before the apple is plucked.

The result is an image full of psychological suspense. It seems to represent a celebration of the uniqueness of their love, but also an unspoken premonition of shame and suffering. We can surely sense that suspense in the figures themselves. They relate slightly awkwardly to each other. Suzanne as Eve seems calm and focused; she is poised elegantly as she reaches out for the apple. Adam – aka André – holds a more awkward pose. His feet take him one way, his shoulders another and his eyes are lost in a 1,000-yard stare.

Their interlocking limbs seem to bind the pair together. Utter has clasped one of Suzanne's hands behind his back as though this is a slight pause in a complicated dance move that locks them together in the face of fate. His other arm stretches round her shoulders and gently grasps her wrist. Is he offering her support, or trying to stop her from eating the apple?

It's a moot question, especially as there is something missing from the painting: there is no silver-tongued serpent, no Satan in the apple tree. Is the implication that Suzanne and André are the authors of their own potential downfall? Or is there no shame to be feared in their earthly paradise? Valadon leaves the questions unanswered. But she is also presenting the scene in a highly provocative and original way. Not only is she appropriating a religious image, she is making a revolutionary cultural statement. This is thought to be the first painting of a naked couple made by a woman. Just as Eve disobeyed God's instructions, Valadon is transgressing the unwritten rules of Western art. And when it was first made, it was even more shocking because Utter was originally depicted without the fig leaves round his waist. These were added later to avoid offending public sensibilities when the painting was exhibited at the Paris Salon (a major exhibition of contemporary art) in 1920.

So it seems that this picture was a highly self-conscious attempt by Valadon to come to terms with what was, even in the heady atmosphere of Belle Époque Paris, a controversial relationship. Suzanne was a married 43-year-old woman and Utter was just 23. They may have felt themselves to be living in a personal paradise, but they risked public opprobrium. As Utter wrote years later: 'how beautiful everything was – except for the gossips'! [49]

Suzanne Valadon was not, however, accustomed to living by conventional rules. Uneducated and untrained, she had hauled herself out of poverty in the 1880s to become one of the most sought-after artists' models of her time. Puvis de Chavannes, Renoir, Degas and Toulouse-Lautrec (with whom she had an

They may have felt themselves to be living in a personal paradise.

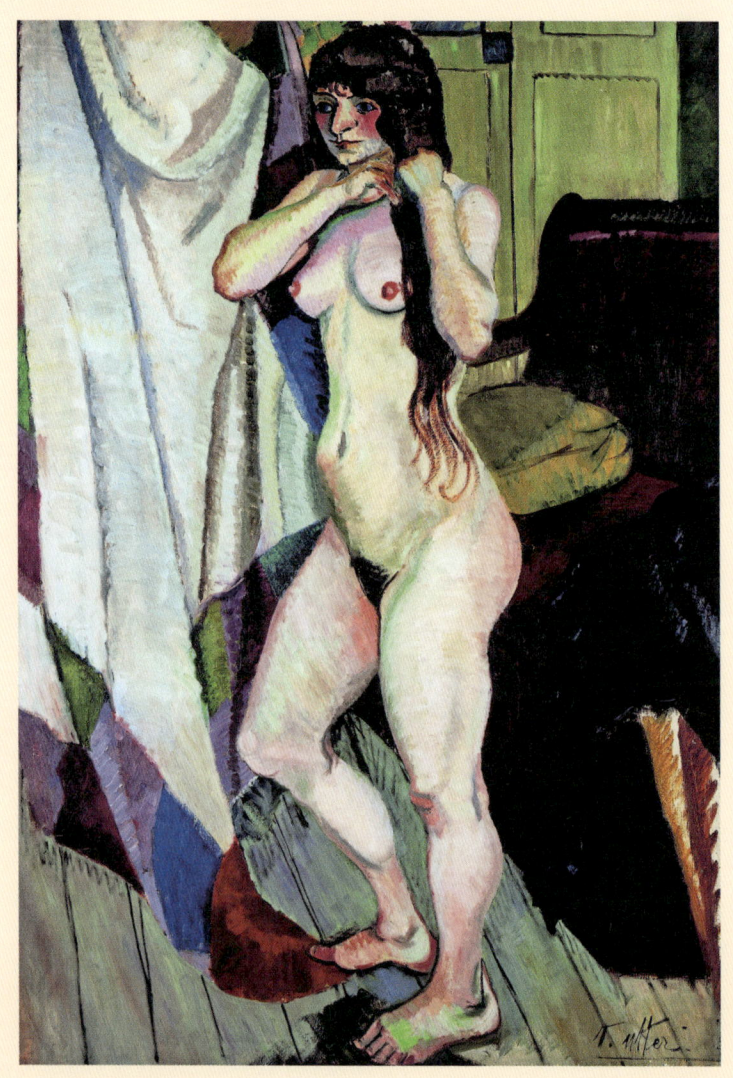

Suzanne Valadon, combing, André Utter, 1913

intense affair) were all obsessed by her. In 1883 she also had
an illegitimate son – Maurice Utrillo (1883–1955) – who also
became an artist, but turned out to be a troubled soul and an
alcoholic, wracked by self-doubt. And she made an ill-fated
marriage to a prosperous stockbroker, Paul Mousis.

In the meantime, Degas recognized her talent as an artist
in her own right and encouraged her to draw and paint. Such was
her progress that, in 1894, five of her drawings were accepted for
exhibition at the salon of the National Society of Fine Arts in
Paris – making her the first woman artist ever to achieve this
level of recognition.

Then, in 1906, she met André Utter. The son of a
Montmartre plumber and a good friend of her son, Maurice, he
also had ambitions to become an artist. Despite the age gap, the
chemistry between him and Suzanne was electric. At their first
meeting, she seemed 'both amazon and fairy,' [50] he said later.

In a delicious reversal of the traditional seduction
of female models by male artists – which she herself had
experienced – Suzanne asked him to pose nude for her. It seems
the temptation of the situation was too much for both of them.
A flurry of erotic bliss followed, during which Suzanne painted
several nudes with Utter as her model. He reciprocated with his
own colourful, slightly clunky tribute. They married in 1914,
after her divorce was finalized, and for years they cohabited with
Maurice. Valadon and Maurice went on to enjoy significant
artistic success, with Utter acting as their agent. But the path of
true love was not smooth: André's relationship with Suzanne
was riven with tensions and jealousies and he eventually began to
take other lovers. By the early 1930s, Suzanne was largely living
alone and in 1934, when she was almost 70, she and Utter finally
separated. Their souls remained entwined, however. Although
André outlived her by 10 years, he was buried alongside her in
Montmartre's Saint-Ouen Cemetery.

Observatory Time, The Lovers, Man Ray, 1932–1934

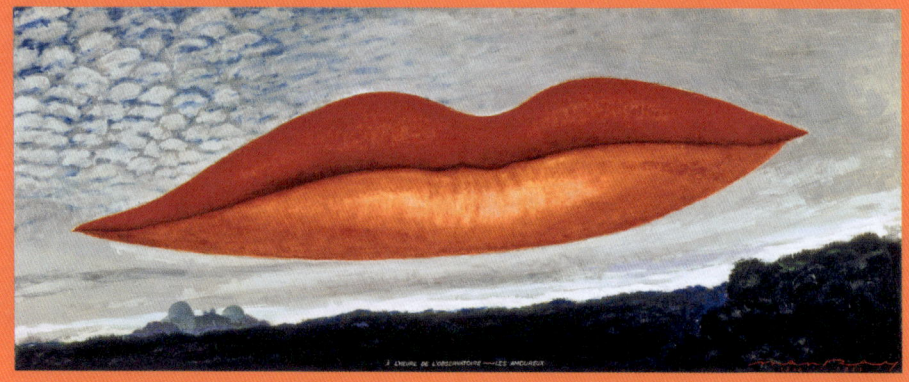

The Anatomy of Love

Lee Miller & Man Ray

A pair of giant, disembodied lips floats over the horizon like a strange, elongated balloon in the cloud-flecked sky of a summer's evening. This painting, by Man Ray, is one of the strangest of the many strange images produced in the early days of the surrealist movement, drawn – apparently – from the realms of dreams and science fiction.

In fact, these are the lips of Man Ray's former lover, the model and photographer, Lee Miller, who had just ended their three-year affair. It is by far the most emotionally resonant of the many images their relationship inspired. At least, it was for Ray. Obsessed by the memory of what he had lost, he saw in the outline of those lips the shape of two lovers embracing.

But they are also a sort of sun. A prose poem, which Man Ray wrote about the painting in 1935, included the line: 'Lips of the sun, you draw me endlessly nearer ...' [51] They had become the centre of his universe, the source of life and the measure of time. This interpretation is reinforced by the title which Man Ray gave to the painting: *Observatory Time, The Lovers*. The observatory is the building on the horizon just below the lips. It is modelled on the Paris Observatory, the point at which French time was set, which he saw every day during his walks in the Jardin du Luxembourg. Even here, the eroticism of the relationship still clearly played on his mind. He likened the outline, with its twin domes, to 'breasts dimly indicated on the horizon'. 'Quite Freudian,' [52] he added. Sometimes – it seems – the full, obsessive force of love isn't experienced until it is over.

It had been a powerful attraction. When she arrived in Paris in 1929, Lee Miller was already a successful New York model who had appeared on the cover of *American Vogue* at the age of 19. Determined to become a photographer, she crossed the Atlantic and introduced herself to one of the most famous of his time, Man Ray. The chemistry between them, both creative and physical, was immediate and the photographs they took over the following three years mark one of the high-points in the development of the art form.

Much of the early emphasis – no doubt fuelled by their passion – was on images of Miller's body. *Lee Miller* is typical of many of the erotic pictures taken by Man Ray which emphasize her sexuality, using light and shade, focus and blur to seduce the eye. He also, slightly spookily perhaps, obsessed about details: as well as photographing her lips, he isolated her neck, torso and eye as separate studies.

Miller made nude self-portraits, too, but when she turned the camera on Ray, the result was more complex. Her early photograph of him in profile, topless, with his chin covered in shaving cream creates a palpable tension. It captures the inherent contradictions between humour and seriousness, intimacy and estrangement in both their love and art. Is this a man about to raise a razor to his throat with infinite care, or a clown applying his make-up?

I say estrangement because their relationship was a tempestuous one and its intensity quickly fell out of kilter. Miller soon began to seek more independence and enjoyed spending time with other men. Man Ray's infatuation, and his angst, only grew stronger. In a letter written to her when she was in London in 1932, he is riven with jealousy and tortured by self-loathing: 'you are so young and beautiful and free and I hate myself for

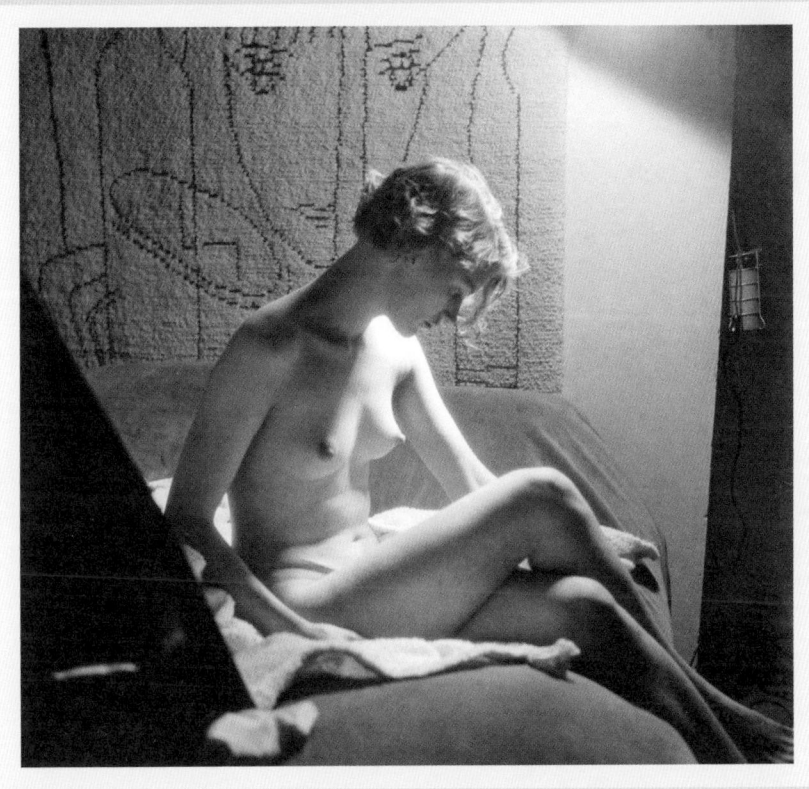

Lee Miller, Man Ray, c.1930

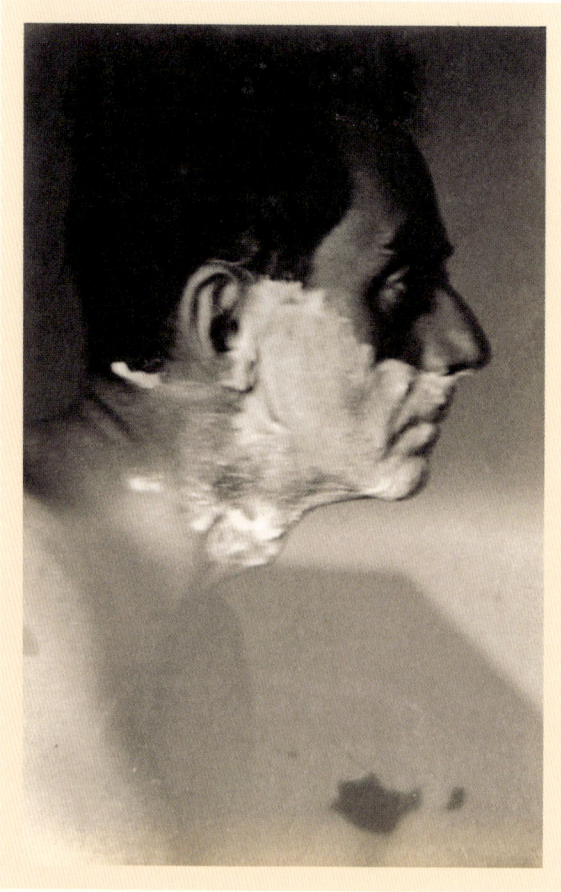

Man Ray shaving, Lee Miller, 1929

trying to cramp that in you which I admire most.'[53] His state of mind – more like that of a lovelorn teenager than a 41-year-old man – is also revealed by a page in his notebook: a sketch of her face is obsessively and repeatedly overwritten by her name.

Later that year, Lee Miller abruptly left Paris. The love affair was over, but for Ray the obsession was not. It was then, rejected and dejected, that he turned to his art to try to find some solace. He had always insisted that painting – a slower, more reflective, more adaptable art form – was more important to him than photography. And it is clearly true that, while photographs can capture brilliantly moments of fun, inventiveness and excitement in a relationship, it is harder to use a camera to explore the complexities of love – or, in this case, lost love.

So Ray hung an eight-foot-wide canvas above his bed and sketched out that giant pair of lips, based on an image he had taken of Lee Miller's mouth three years earlier. First thing each morning, he would stand on the mattress and continue to work on the painting.

It took him two years to complete and even then his intoxication seems undiminished. In fact, it had transformed into a sort of dream-like adoration. His poem about the painting included the line: 'I am weightless – I meet you in the even light and empty space, and, my only reality, kiss you with all that is left of me: my own lips.'[54]

La Belle Rafaela, Tamara de Lempicka, 1927

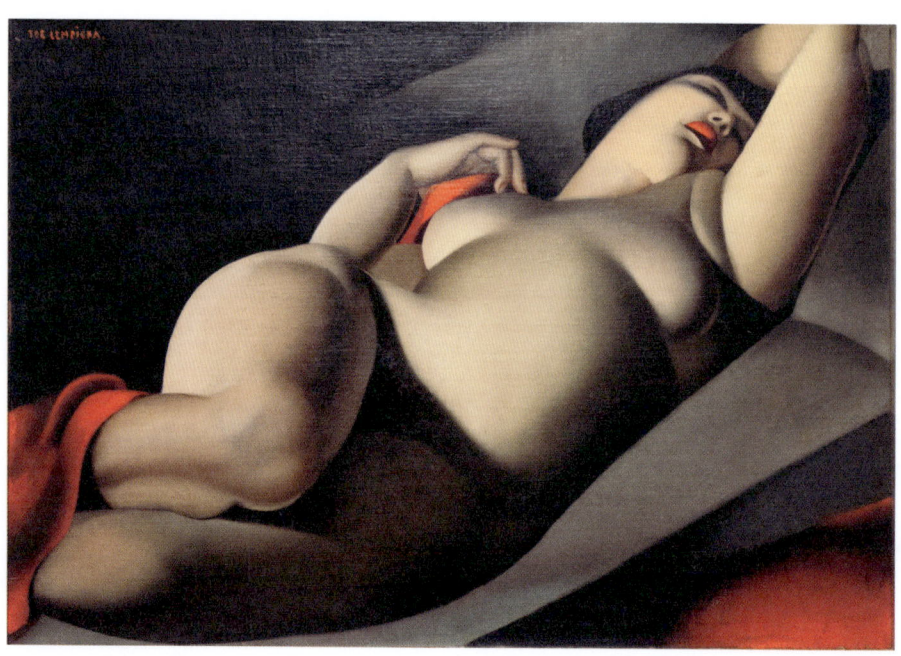

A Walk in the Park

Tamara de Lempicka & Rafaela

'She is the most beautiful woman I have ever seen – huge black eyes, beautiful sensuous mouth, beautiful body. I stop her and say to her, "Mademoiselle, I'm a painter and I would like you to pose for me. Would you do this?" She says "Yes. Why not?"' [55]

This is Tamara de Lempicka's description – as recorded by her daughter Kizette – of the time she met a young woman called Rafaela in the Bois de Boulogne on the outskirts of Paris. Tamara immediately took her home to her studio and, after lunch, they got to work.

It was, at first at least, an entirely straightforward arrangement. De Lempicka told her to undress and lie down on the sofa. 'She lay. Every position was art – perfection and I started to paint her, and I painted her for over a year.' [56] We know very little else about her, except that she was most probably a prostitute – the Bois de Boulogne was a well-known pick-up place. Lempicka never revealed Rafaela's surname and her identity is lost to history. But we do know that she painted her at least six times over that year, sometimes naked, always voluptuous, always tantalizingly erotic.

La Belle Rafaela is the most famous and most sensually abandoned of those portraits. In fact, it is barely a portrait.

Lost in her own rapture, Rafaela has been distilled into an object of desire. Not only are we being allowed an intimate, almost voyeuristic panorama of her body as she stretches out in languorous ecstasy, but Lempicka thrusts her towards us: so close that she doesn't quite fit into the frame; so close that we feel we could almost reach out and touch her. Yet she remains apparently unaware of – or at least unconcerned by – her audience.

It is also a painting of high theatricality. There is the dramatic contrast of light and shade, which highlights and simplifies the curves of Rafaela's body and even the pout of her slightly parted lips: lips which are given further prominence by the brilliantly simple palette. It's a composition composed, virtually, in monochrome, with just four bright red highlights that seem to guide our eyes around her body to her mouth – reds that also cast the faintest orange-pink blush on her skin. But the drama is tempered by the softness of the curves, the luminosity of Rafaela's skin and the tenderness and sensuality of the gentle touch of her fingertips on her own breast. It all adds up to a sense of extraordinary gentleness and allure.

When Tamara de Lempicka made this picture in 1927, she was in her early 30s. An emigrée from revolutionary Russia who was married to an impoverished Polish nobleman, she was a party animal who moved in the highest circles of bohemian Paris. She had started to make a name for herself as an artist through her stylish and distinctive portraits which captured the glamorous atmosphere of the 1920s. And she was already experimenting with female nudes – a subject that was to obsess her throughout her artistic life. In the mid 1920s, this was still a highly unconventional and provocative thing for a woman to do (see p90) and she often signed them with the male form of her surname (Lempitzki) to mask the fact that she was a woman.

There is no doubt that Lempicka was bisexual and that she enjoyed the interaction with her nude models. She also had many affairs with both men and women which she did little to hide (though she almost never painted naked men). Her portrait

'Every
position was
art ... I started
to paint her, and
I painted her
for over
a year.'

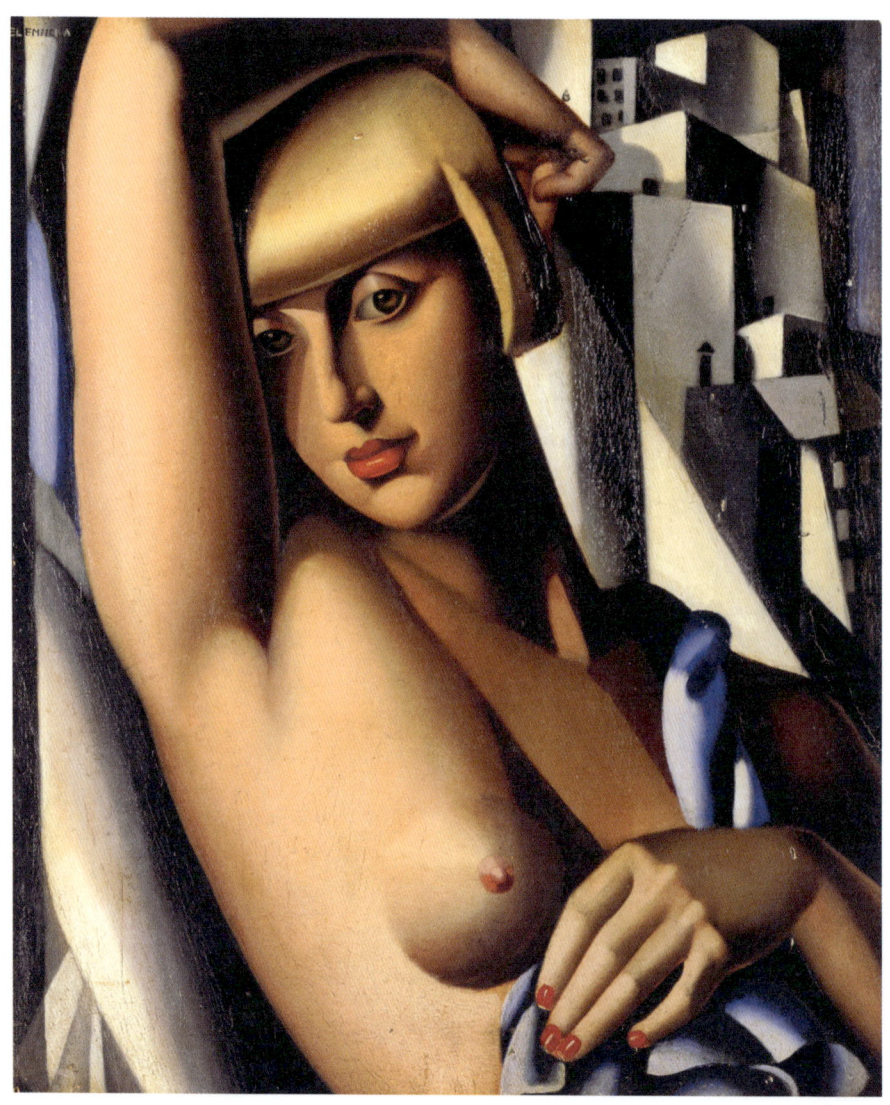

Portrait of Suzy Solidor, Tamara de Lempicka, 1933

of Suzy Solidor, the owner of a famous lesbian nightclub La Vie Parisienne, was made in 1933 and is a memento of one of her most ardent flings. Just as with Rafaela, she painted Solidor on condition that she posed naked.

But did she seduce Rafaela herself? Is *La Belle Rafaela* also a tribute to another passionate affair or is it a testament to unfulfilled desire? There is no objective proof either way. Lempicka never explicitly admitted that the relationship was consummated, but most people have assumed that this must have been the case. After all, her first husband famously complained that she slept with everyone she painted. And there are good reasons why Tamara might well have been reticent about confirming a physical affair with a prostitute. She was a highly liberated woman, but this was one social taboo for women which she was almost certainly wary of breaking.

Given the explicitly erotic language with which Lempicka describes her encounter with Rafaela, surely this is a case when we can rely on what art tells us about love or at least about desire. The sense of the artist's infatuation is palpable. We also know that the last painting that Tamara was working on when she died in 1980 was a copy of that 1927 painting of Rafaela. The woman she met in the park more than half a century earlier was still stirring memories.

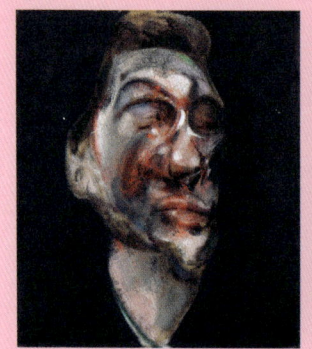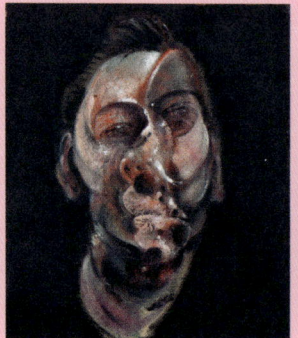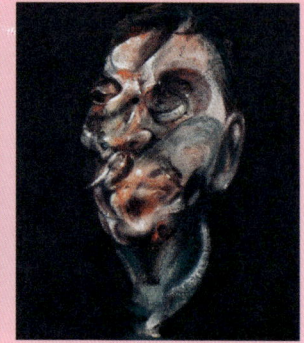

Three Studies for Portrait of George Dyer, Francis Bacon, 1963

Torment &
Tragedy

Francis Bacon & George Dyer

'An artist must be nourished by his passions and his despairs',[57] said Francis Bacon (1909–1992). And the greatest passion in his life and the greatest source of despair was George Dyer (1934–1971), his lover and model for most of the 1960s. *Three Studies for Portrait of George Dyer* is the first painting Bacon made of him, a couple of months after they met in London in 1963. He was a muscular man – a petty East End criminal with a slightly menacing air. Bacon was 24 years older and already a hugely successful international artist. Bacon liked to romanticize their first meeting, claiming that he disturbed Dyer breaking into his house. In reality, they got talking during a drunken evening in a Soho pub and Bacon, who was always excited by a sense of edginess and risk, was deeply attracted to the younger man.

Presenting the head of his subject in two different profiles flanking a full-frontal portrait, the triptych is a typical model for the approach he used for both portraits and self-portraits. It creates, quite literally, a composite three-dimensional image, giving it a sculptural quality, here enhanced by the way Dyer's head seems to loom out of a pitch-black background.

One of Bacon's gifts was that he was able to distort a face or a body, yet still capture a recognizable likeness. In these

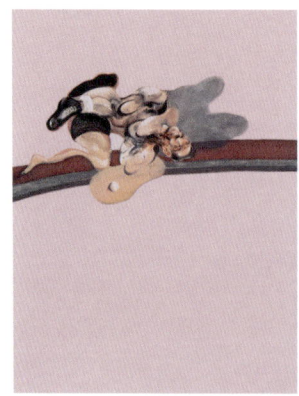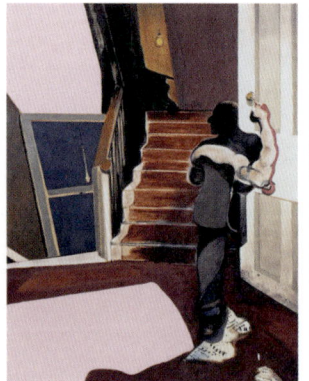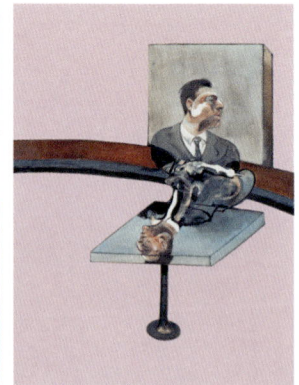

In Memory of George Dyer, Francis Bacon, 1971

paintings he goes a step further. We can make out the face of George Dyer but, especially in the right-hand portrait, there are also aspects of Bacon's own physiognomy. It is as though the two faces are merging in a sort of spiritual and physical union.[58] Meanwhile, in the left-hand image, Dyer's closed eyes suggest something of the erotic intimacy they had discovered together. As Bacon said: 'the creative process is ... a mixture of consciousness and unconsciousness, of fear and pleasure; it's a little like making love, the physical act of love.' [59]

Yet although the triptych was made in the heat of those passionate first few months of their relationship, it hardly has the air of an adoring and devoted tribute to Bacon's newfound obsession. There is coldness here as well as desire, especially in the glassy-eyed stare and ugly distortion of Dyer's nose in the central panel. And it was only the beginning of Bacon's attempts to capture what Dyer meant to him. He went on to make more than 40 portraits of 'Sir George', as he called him. But while the relationship was always a rich source of inspiration for Bacon's art, it was not a healthy one for either partner. Over the next seven years, Dyer struggled to cope with his role and status in Bacon's highly sophisticated, if often drunken, social and intellectual milieu, who soon got bored with the idea of Dyer as a sort of loveable rogue.

By the late 1960s, Bacon had begun to find him more and more tiresome and Dyer became increasingly alienated and deeply dependent on alcohol. In October 1971, two evenings before the first Bacon retrospective in France opened in the Grand Palais in Paris, Dyer was found dead from an overdose of drink and drugs, sitting on the lavatory of their hotel room.[60] Bacon managed to continue with the exhibition opening, but as soon as he returned to London, he started work on the monumental triptych *In Memory of George Dyer* which he finished in December. Made as he emerged from shock and grief, it is the first of several works that enshrine his artistic response to his lover's death, works in which Dyer's presence continues to burn in Bacon's imagination.

The central scene depicts Dyer in black, shadow-like profile as though he were haunting the staircase of Bacon's studio. The steps lead up to a mysterious room lit by a light bulb and where another shadow seems to lurk. It has the air of a ghost-like exit to another world, yet the shadow is disrupted in a slightly disturbing way by real flesh. A muscled arm emerges from the wrong place and in the wrong direction from the shadow, the hand attached to it seemingly inserting a key into the door lock.

To the left, Dyer is a boxer floored with upturned head and blank unseeing eyes against the curving skirting board. Is there a memory here of Bacon's discovery of his body in the hotel room? Certainly those memories figure in later triptychs. Finally, the right-hand painting is a confusing montage in which Dyer's profile, reflected in a mirror, seems to collapse into a blurred mess of paint. It then recomposes itself, facing in the opposite direction, on a table or, perhaps, a canvas lying on the table. It is only weeks since Dyer's death, yet in these canvases Bacon seems to be separating out three dimensions of their relationship: the physical, the spiritual and, perhaps most important from an artistic point of view, the inspirational.

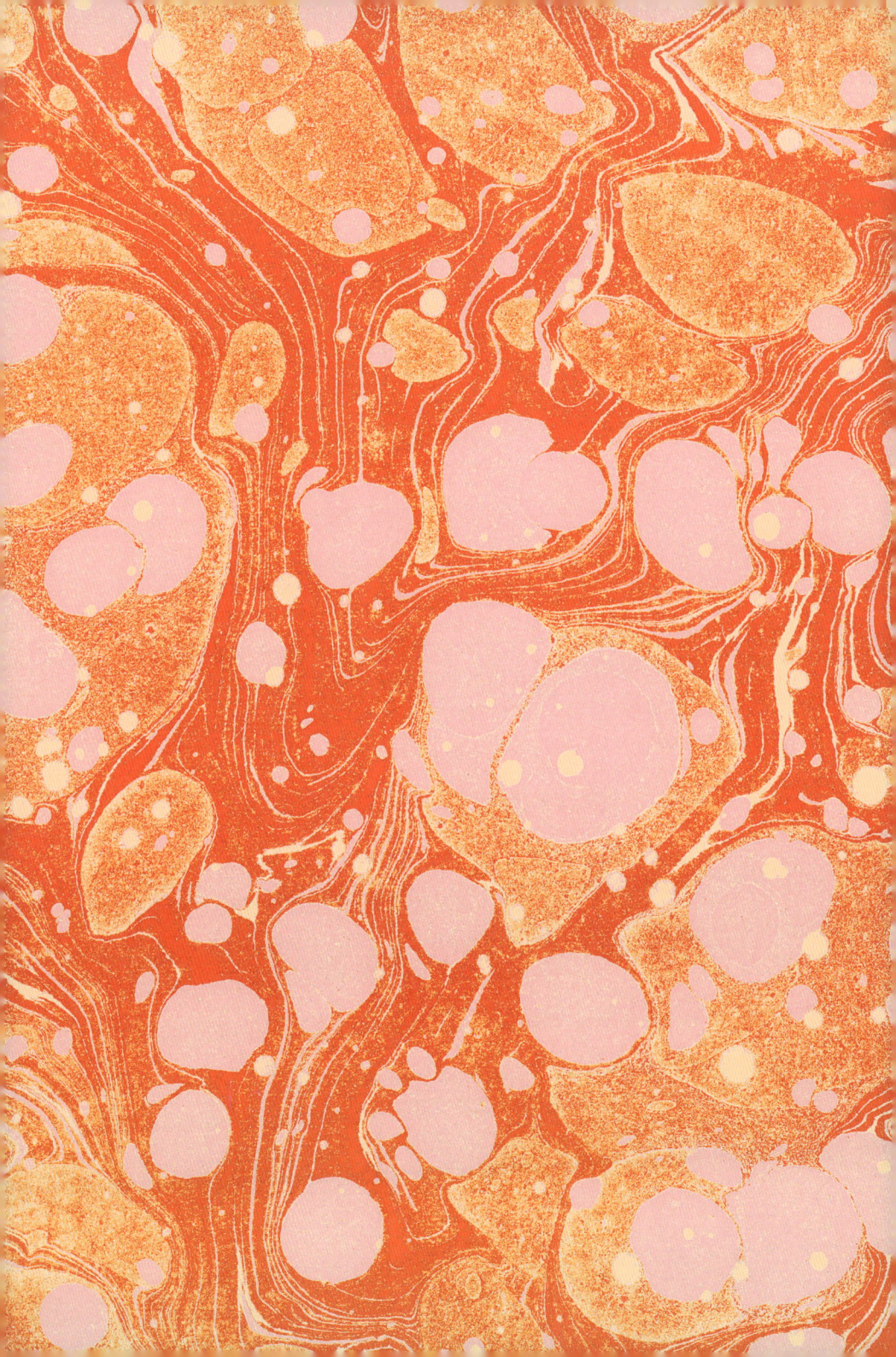

LOVE

TRIANGLES

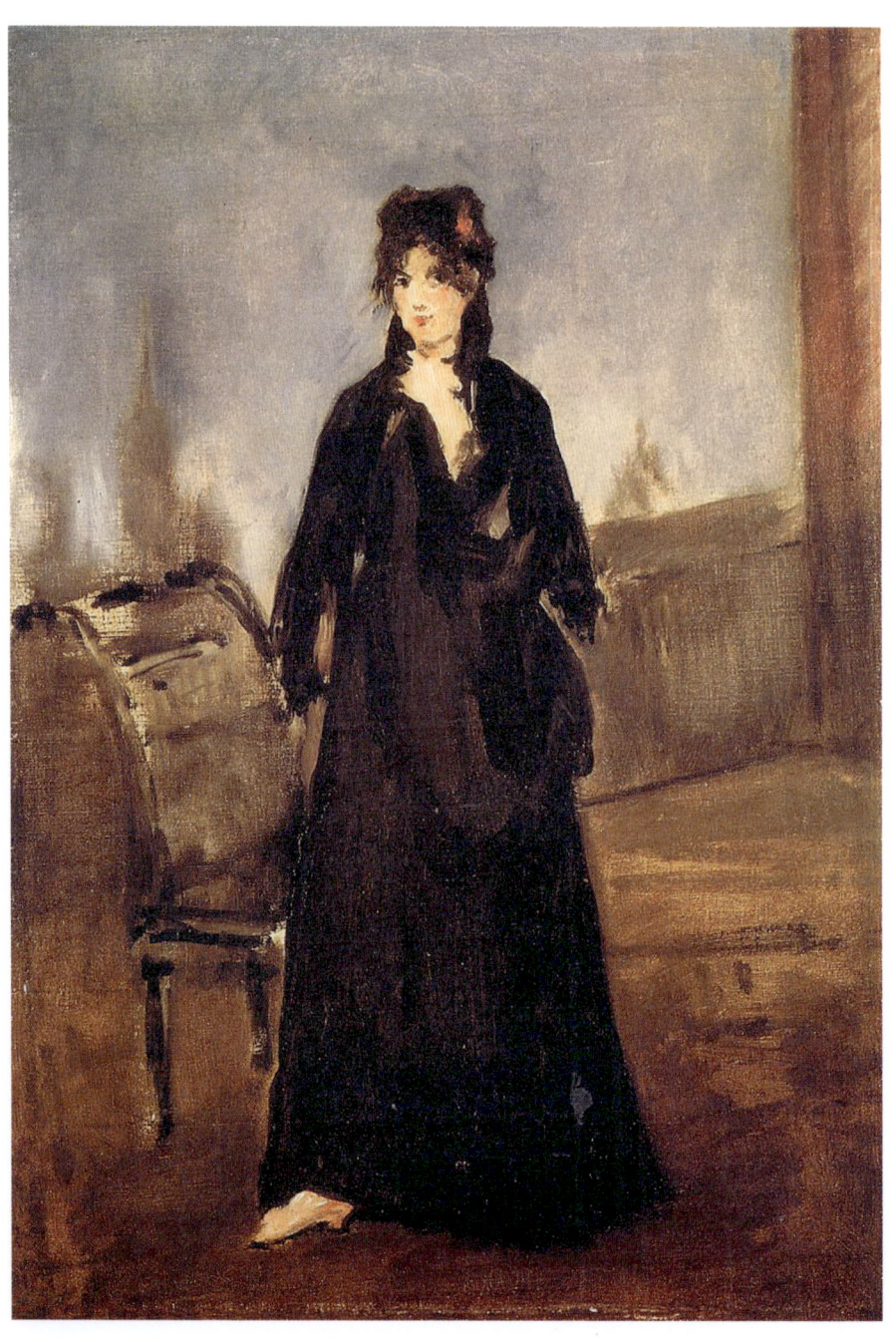

Portrait of Berthe Morisot in Pink Shoes, Édouard Manet, 1872

Torn Between Two Brothers

Berthe Morisot & the Manets

'Seductive women always turn their feet out. Don't expect to get anywhere with a woman who turns her feet in,' Édouard Manet once remarked to the poet, Stéphane Mallarmé.[61] In the light of that blatant misogyny, how should we judge Manet's portrait of the artist Berthe Morisot whose right foot, strikingly emphasized by the bright pink slipper, is so decidedly turned out? We don't know who chose the pose. Probably they each had their say, but it seems doubtful that Morisot had a clear insight into Manet's foot fetish. He was married but a notorious womanizer; she was a single woman from a respectable, well-connected family.

Yet despite the social constraints around women's sexual freedom, they were both moving in bohemian artistic circles, and Berthe certainly seems to have been aware of a sensual frisson to the pink shoes, which were a favourite of hers. The Morisot family believed themselves to be indirect descendants of the 18th-century artist, Jean-Honoré Fragonard, who was also greatly admired by Manet, and with whom Morisot's work was often compared.[62] One of Fragonard's most famous paintings, *The Happy Accidents of the Swing,* had been in the public eye a few years earlier when it was sold at auction in Paris in 1865. It is an extremely risqué picture in which a young woman is rising high on a swing while a voyeur looks up her skirts. She is aware of the situation and – as she reaches the peak, in a moment of flirtatious abandon – she lifts her leg and kicks off her bright pink shoe.

Berthe's pink shoe is not the only frisson in Manet's portrait. As Berthe raises her left hand to her throat, apparently to adjust her neck band, her sleeve falls down revealing her forearm. But at first glance, and given the loose nature of the brushstrokes, the viewer may be confused. The exposed skin makes it seem as though her dress is open at the neck. There is something disorienting about the background, too. Manet has sketched it only roughly, in neutral colours, but the lines of perspective seem to tip the room towards us, just as the chair appears to rock back slightly. It all feels a little destabilized and the only points of certainty are that shoe and Berthe's steady gaze, which meets our eyes so directly.

Manet – then one of the best-known and most provocative painters in Paris – had met Berthe, who was 19 years younger and just beginning her career, in 1868. The families became friends. The two artists got along famously and were inspired by each other's work. In that same year, Manet used Berthe as the model for the dark-eyed beauty who sits in the foreground of a painting called *The Balcony*. Two figures stand behind her, while another is half hidden in the background gloom. Her appearance in the picture won her the reputation of a femme fatale.

Parisian life was badly disrupted by war and insurrection in 1870 and 1871. But after that, Manet was to paint her 11 more times in less than three years[63], including a few fervent months after he moved to a new studio at 4 rue Saint-Pétersbourg. She would visit him by carriage and, during this time, he made six portraits of her, including *Portrait of Berthe Morisot in Pink Shoes*. It all amounts to a remarkably intense artistic outpouring and it was laced with personal intimacies.

Did they have a physical relationship? There is no proof apart from the emotional connection which seems to infuse these paintings and one fascinating clue: as well as painting her portrait

Bouquet of Violets, Édouard Manet, 1872

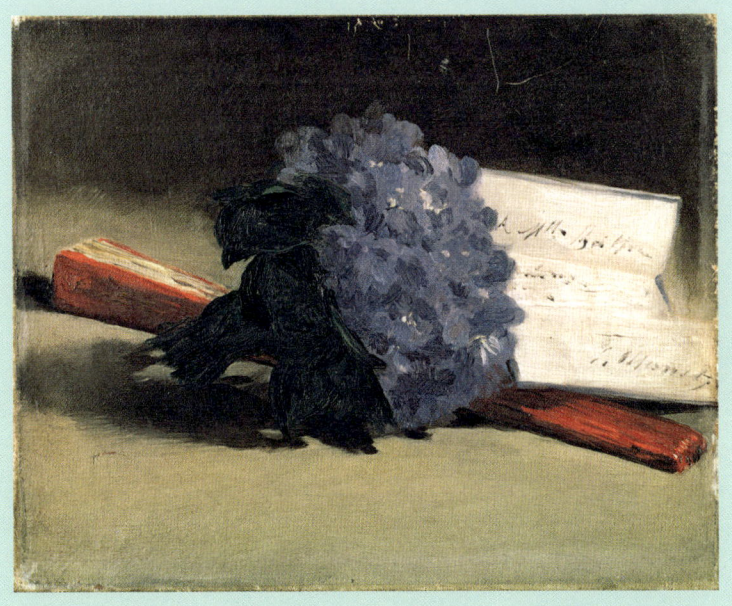

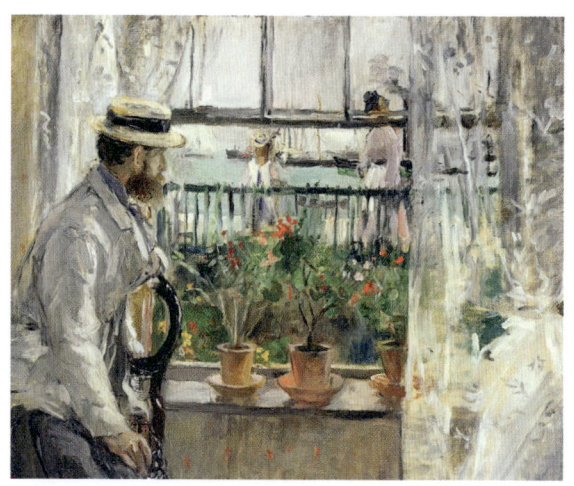

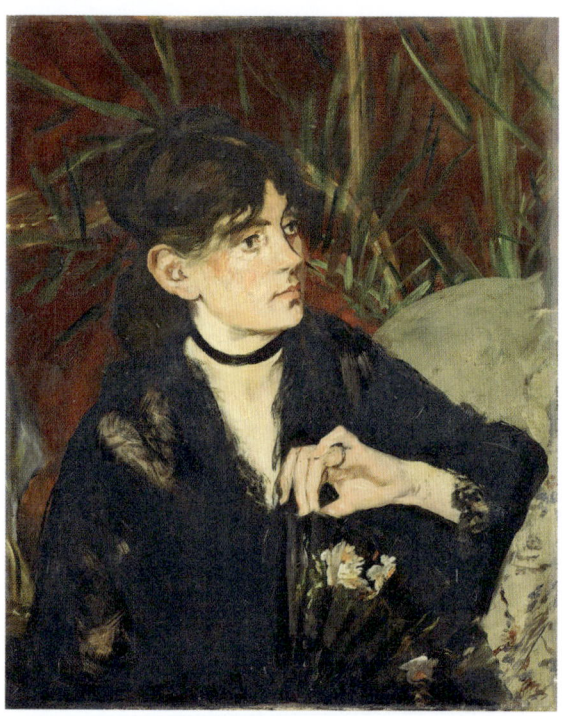

(Top) *Eugène Manet on the Isle of Wight*, Berthe Morisot, 1875
(Above) *Berthe Morisot with a Fan*, Édouard Manet, 1874

over and over again, in 1872 Manet also gave Berthe a little picture, *Bouquet of Violets*. It contains a depiction of a half-folded letter, addressed to her and signed by Manet, though otherwise illegible. It lies next to the fan she held in *The Balcony* and a bunch of violets, like the one she was holding in another portrait he made of her earlier that year. It is clearly a deeply sentimental memento of shared intimacies and there may be further significance in the violets themselves. That different flowers could symbolize different emotions or qualities was a highly popular idea. But traditions varied: violets could represent either virtue or secret love. Perhaps for Manet and Morisot they symbolized the tension between the two.

There are also signs of Manet's emotional turmoil in the last portraits he made of Berthe. In 1874, her father died and, soon after, aged 33, she agreed to marry Manet's brother Eugène. Édouard's response was extraordinary. He painted just two more portraits of her. In both, she seems a haunted shadow of her former, exuberant self. It is as though a fire has gone out. Of course, she was in mourning, but in the final portrait (opposite) she looks away from the viewer. The black fan in her right hand is open and she is holding up her left hand and lifting her little finger, apparently to display her engagement ring. Édouard never painted her again.

Berthe never attempted Édouard's portrait, but she did depict her husband several times. There is no passion in the paintings, however, which don't suggest a profound connection, rather a partnership of convenience. Eugène was, Berthe complained in her letters, an impatient model and this comes out in his stiff, awkward postures. The painting she made during a visit to Cowes on the Isle of Wight in 1885 is typical (opposite). Eugène, turned away from the viewer, seems tense and distracted and his significance within the painting is subtly diminished. His hat band seems to become part of the window frame and his jacket blends with the curtains. It couldn't be more different from his brother's paintings of Berthe.

Portrait of Frau Martha Dix, Otto Dix, 1923

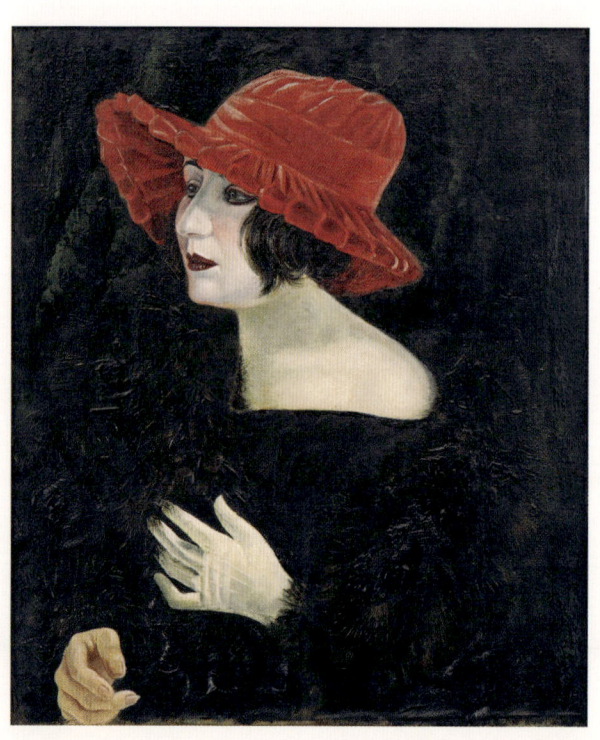

Love Invisible

Otto Dix, Martha & Käthe

An extract from a letter written in 1948 gives a revealing insight into the complicated mind – and the complicated life – of the German artist, Otto Dix (1891–1969): 'I have never written any confessions of mine, since, as you will see, my paintings are confessions of the most sincere kind ... He who has eyes to see, let him see!' [64] It is an especially interesting diktat to apply to his double life – his relationships with his wife Martha (he always called her Mutzli), whom he married in 1923, and his lifelong but secret affair with Käthe König, which began in 1927.

The portrait of Martha in a red velvet hat is the first formal painting he made of his new wife. It's a remarkably intense picture, replete with a subtle play of tones and colours. The reds of her lips and cheeks are emphasized by her hat. The blacks of her eyes echo those of her dress, her hair and the warm fur which she gathers around herself. The pale skin of her exposed shoulder contrasts with the thick white powder on her face and the soft, creamy coloured leather of one gloved hand, with the bare flesh of the other. All these resonances are offset by the dark green curtain that forms the backdrop.

It amounts to a lush, warm, deeply tactile image and – most fascinating of all – it is also in stark contrast to the other paintings he had been making since the end of the First World

'As you
will see, my
paintings are
confessions
of the most
sincere
kind.'

War. His portraits were typically high caricatures, sometimes to the point of cruelty, and he had also been obsessed by the brutal imagery of battle, sex and death. His early work as a young artist in Dresden had sometimes revealed his dark side, but nearly four years as a machine gunner on the Western Front was a trauma from which his imagination never recovered.

Martha Koch offered some respite from such memories. Dix had met her in October 1921 when she was married to Dr Hans Koch, a Düsseldorf urologist who had commissioned Otto to paint his portrait. The attraction between Dix and the 26-year-old Martha was immediate and so powerful that when he returned to Dresden, she followed him, leaving her two children behind with her husband. It wasn't quite as brutal as it sounds – Koch was in love with Martha's older sister and he always remained good friends with the runaway lovers. The divorce was finalized in 1922 and Dix and Martha married in February 1923. Eventually, in 1925, the couple moved to Berlin.

Dix continued to paint Martha obsessively – more than 70 paintings, watercolours and drawings of her survive, either alone or as mother to their children, including several of her giving birth.[65] The most striking of the portraits is included in *The Artist's Family* which he made in the spring of 1927. It marks the birth of their second son, Ursus, and is a highly self-conscious reference to Renaissance and medieval religious painting. The subject matter itself suggests an adoration of the baby Jesus by one of the shepherds. The compressed style of the composition – most notably the way Dix's grinning, cross-eyed face (medieval shepherds were often portrayed as crude rustics) has been inserted into the group – is medieval in concept. And the offer, by their eldest child, Nelly, of a red carnation must be a reference to the *Madonna of the Carnation* by Leonardo da Vinci, which Dix could have seen in Munich.

The result is a highly nuanced painting, which grows in complexity the more you look at it. There is a slightly devilish look in the eyes of Ursus. Nelly's direct stare dissociates her from the scene and the offered flower seems to be directed at us rather than the baby. But – and this seems crucial to Dix's perception of his wife – above the interplay of different gazes, of fingers, hands and feet, Martha embraces Ursus and Otto and smiles down on her family benignly.

The idyll was soon to become a mirage. That year the family moved to Dresden where Otto took up a professorship at the Dresden Academy. He quickly fell in love with a local model and legal official, Käthe König. It was a profound and intense relationship which, in 1939, produced a daughter Katharina. But the affair was kept entirely secret from Martha, who only discovered its existence by accident a few weeks before Dix died.

Most fascinatingly, from an artistic point of view, once the affair began, Dix stopped painting Martha. The last two formal portraits date from 1928. Meanwhile, there are no portraits of Käthe. She was invisible in more ways than one, even though the affair endured for decades.

When he was dismissed from his professorship by the Nazis in 1933, and the family moved to Lake Constance, Dix continued to send money and visit Käthe regularly until at least 1966, continuing his visits even during the Cold War. It seems to have been an intensely passionate relationship. Some 785 highly intimate and erotic letters survive but, under German privacy law, they cannot be published until 2040.

If Otto Dix really did feel that his paintings were 'confessions of the most sincere kind', perhaps the secrets and emotional contradictions of his life after he met Käthe were simply too complicated for him to come to terms with through his paintings. In this case, it seems it is not the art, but the lack of it, which tells us about Dix's love.

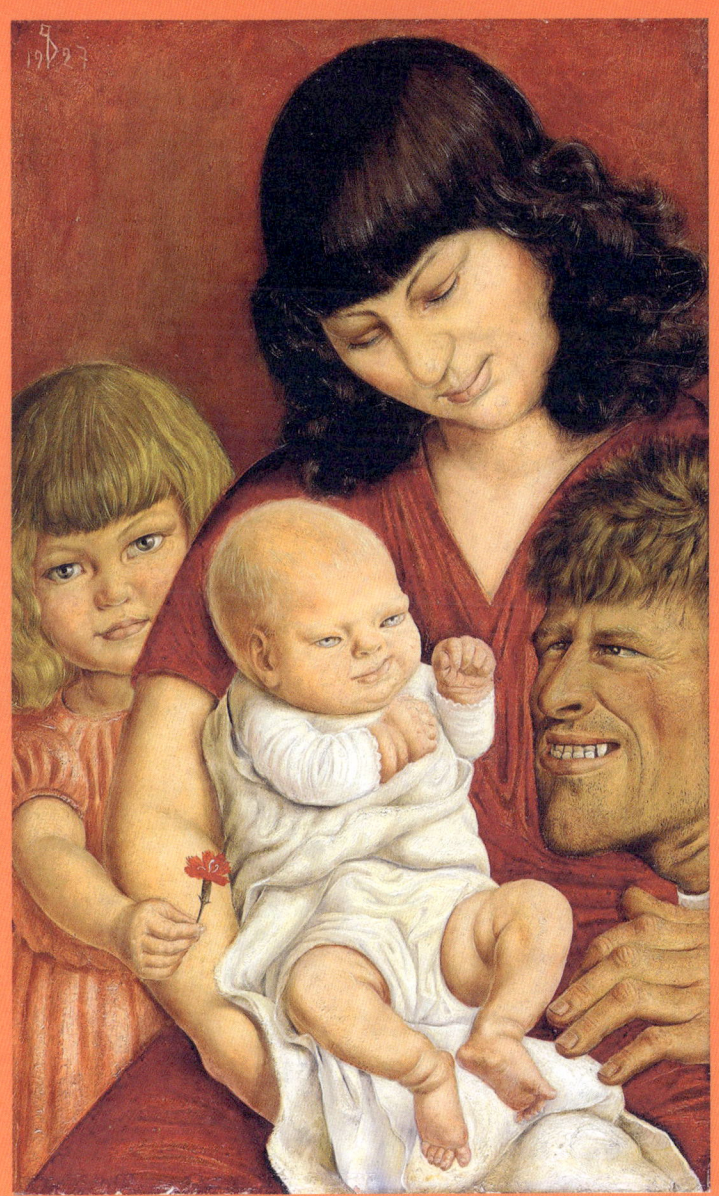

The Artist's Family, Otto Dix, 1927

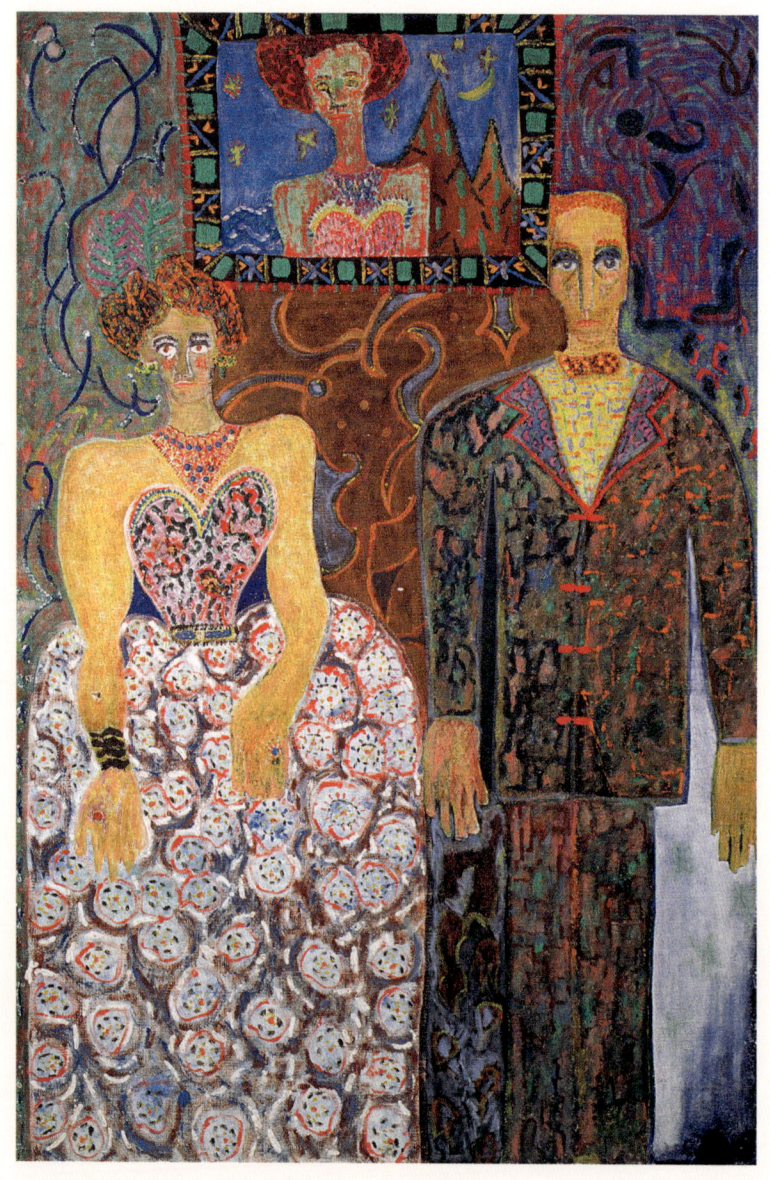

Family Portrait, Niki de Saint Phalle, c.1954–1955

Trauma & Redemption

Niki de Saint Phalle, Harry Mathews & Jean Tinguely

For some artists it can be hard to express love. The art of Niki de Saint Phalle (1930–2002) went through spasms of trauma and violence before she emerged into her celebratory world of colour and warmth. The trauma came first – it seems to bleed through one of her earliest paintings, *Family Portrait* (1954–1955). Made during her pregnancy with her second child, and as part of her recuperation from a mental breakdown, it is a strange, static depiction of a couple – presumably the artist and her first husband, Harry Mathews, though it could also refer to her own parents – stiffened with awkwardness, staring straight ahead, disconnected, untouching. Their cheeks are sunken, their expressions blank, their lips pursed.

There are some notes of optimism. The colours are rich and vibrant, the woman's corset is shaped like the upper part of a love heart and the picture on the wall behind – perhaps the same woman, or her mother or daughter – seems much more optimistic. In that much smaller image, there is a tilt to her head and in the background is a landscape of sea and mountains set against a night sky and a shooting star. It could represent a memory. It might be a dream of escape.

There are good reasons for Saint Phalle's emotional turmoil at the time. Six years earlier, aged just 18, she had eloped

163

with Mathews, a young American writer. It was a passionate affair, but it was also a means of escape from her father who had sexually abused her as a child. Not surprising then, as she tried to process that trauma while nurturing a family of her own, that she should produce such an ambivalent image.

It was only the beginning of a much darker emotional ride, however. The year after she finished *Family Portrait*, she met the charismatic Swiss artist Jean Tinguely and began to discover avant-garde French and American art. By the beginning of 1961, she had left her family. The marriage had been difficult, with affairs on both sides and a tendency for violent outbursts from Saint Phalle. She 'was filled with a resentment of me,' said Mathews. 'It led her to be physically violent and we both had a very upsetting time.' [66]

That aggression found expression in her art. *Portrait of My Lover* (1961) does not identify the subject. 'I was actually very angry with a boyfriend I had and I enjoyed throwing darts at his image', she said.[67] It is a visceral work. The lover's head is a dartboard painted like a target, his torso a paint-spattered shirt nailed to a blackboard. A second version became a performance piece, where viewers were invited to throw darts at the head. It proved to be the precursor of the works which made Saint Phalle famous – her shooting paintings, a more spectacular form of performance art in which Saint Phalle, or an invited guest, used a rifle to shoot at bags of brightly coloured paint which then spattered over a canvas or sculpture or other installation. At the time she was clear about the multiplicity of targets in her imagination: 'I shot at Papa, at all men, at important men, fat men, men, my brother, society, the church, the convent school, my family, my mother ...'.[68]

She was purging herself emotionally. But she soon stepped back from the imagery of violence, revenge and destruction. 'I thought beforehand that to be provocative, you had to attack religion or generals,' she explained later. But then, she said, 'I realised that there was nothing more shocking than joy.' [69]

Portrait of My Lover, Niki de Saint Phalle, 1961

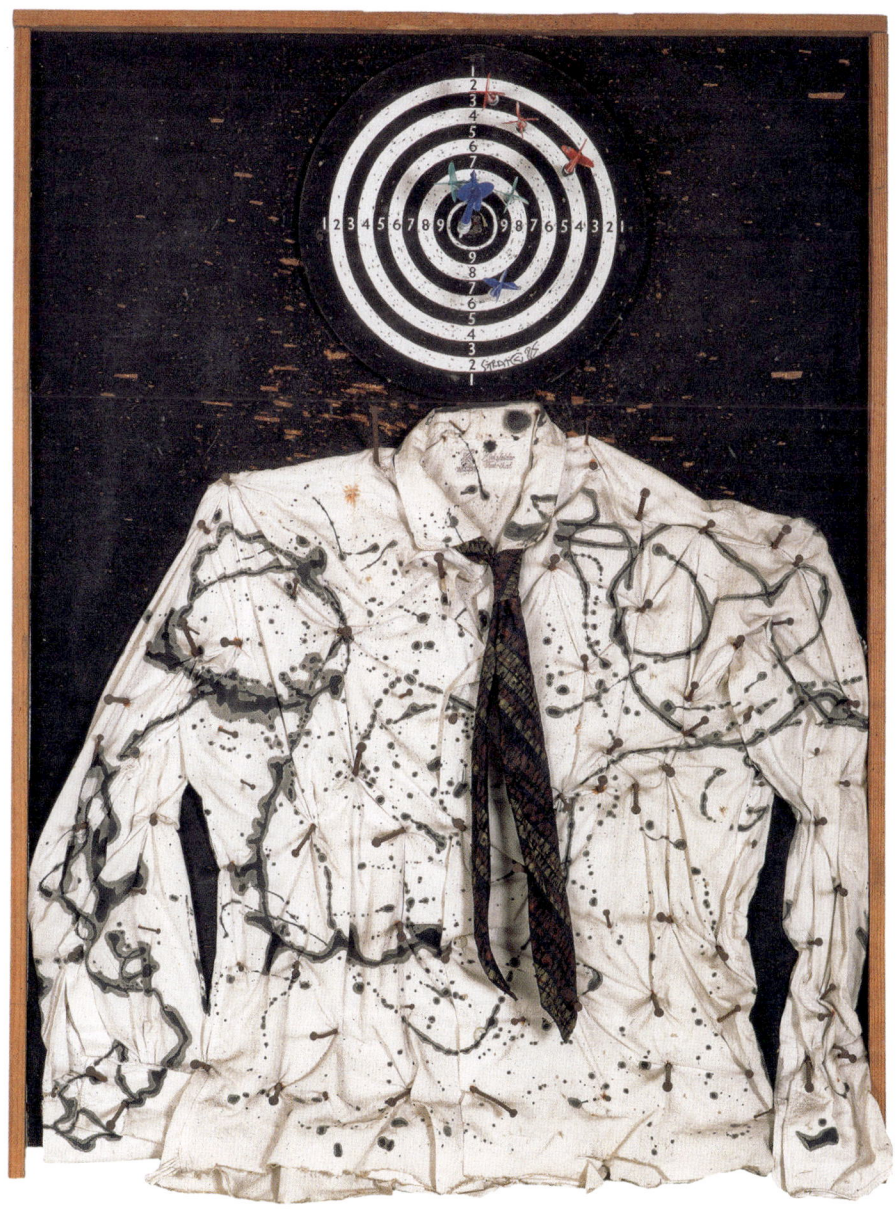

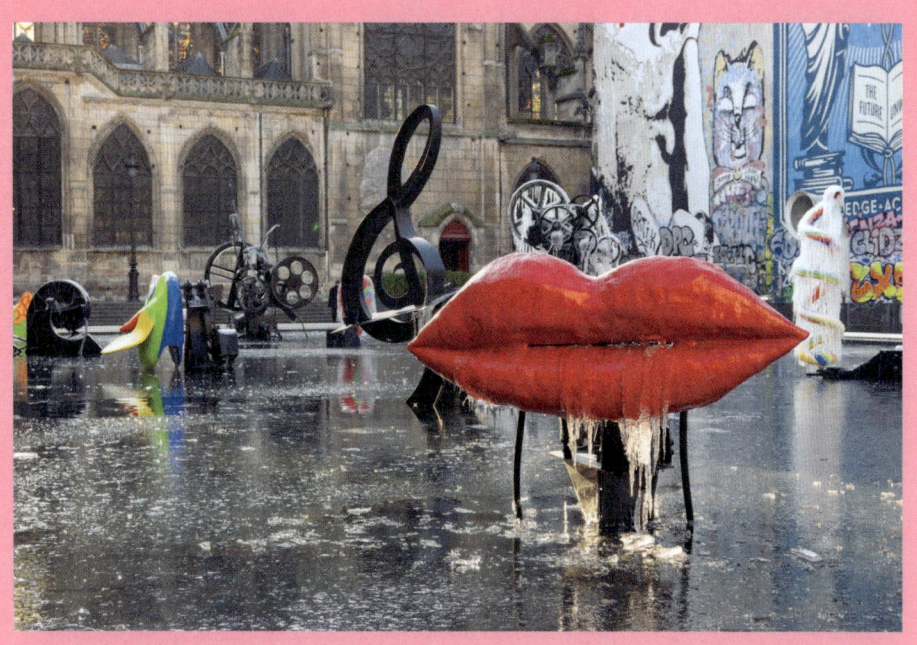

The Stravinsky Fountain, Niki de Saint Phalle and Jean Tinguely, 1983

That joy was rooted in her enduring relationship with Tinguely and encapsulated in her Nana sculptures, which she first began to make in the 1960s. 'Nana' is French slang for a girl, and these girls are exuberant, curvaceous figures, covered in brightly coloured patterns. They come in all sizes and all postures, running, jumping, turning somersaults. Sometimes they are innocent, sometimes sexualized like the giant *She* (1966), which she made with Jean Tinguely and which could be entered through a door between her legs and whose insides included a love nest for visitors.

The colour and positivity of the Nanas also filtered through into a series of faux naive but charming prints and compositions based explicitly on the theme of love. After many years of trauma, bitterness and retribution, her images blossomed into uncomplicated almost childlike celebrations. The screen print *Love Letter to my Lover* is a playful Valentine's card of isolated images and messages, a Valentine's card captioned with the playful clichés of love – 'you are my sun', 'I am yours', 'I give you my body'.

This playful approach was also evident in another joint project she undertook with Tinguely in 1983. The *Stravinsky Fountain* was designed for the Place Stravinsky, next to the Pompidou Centre in Paris. It comprises some 16 whimsical sculptures set in a shallow pool and intended to celebrate Stravinsky's music. Tinguely's contributions are black and move mechanically, while Saint Phalle's are brilliant and colourful. They include a giant pair of bright red lips, spouting a jet of water, which Saint Phalle called *Love*.

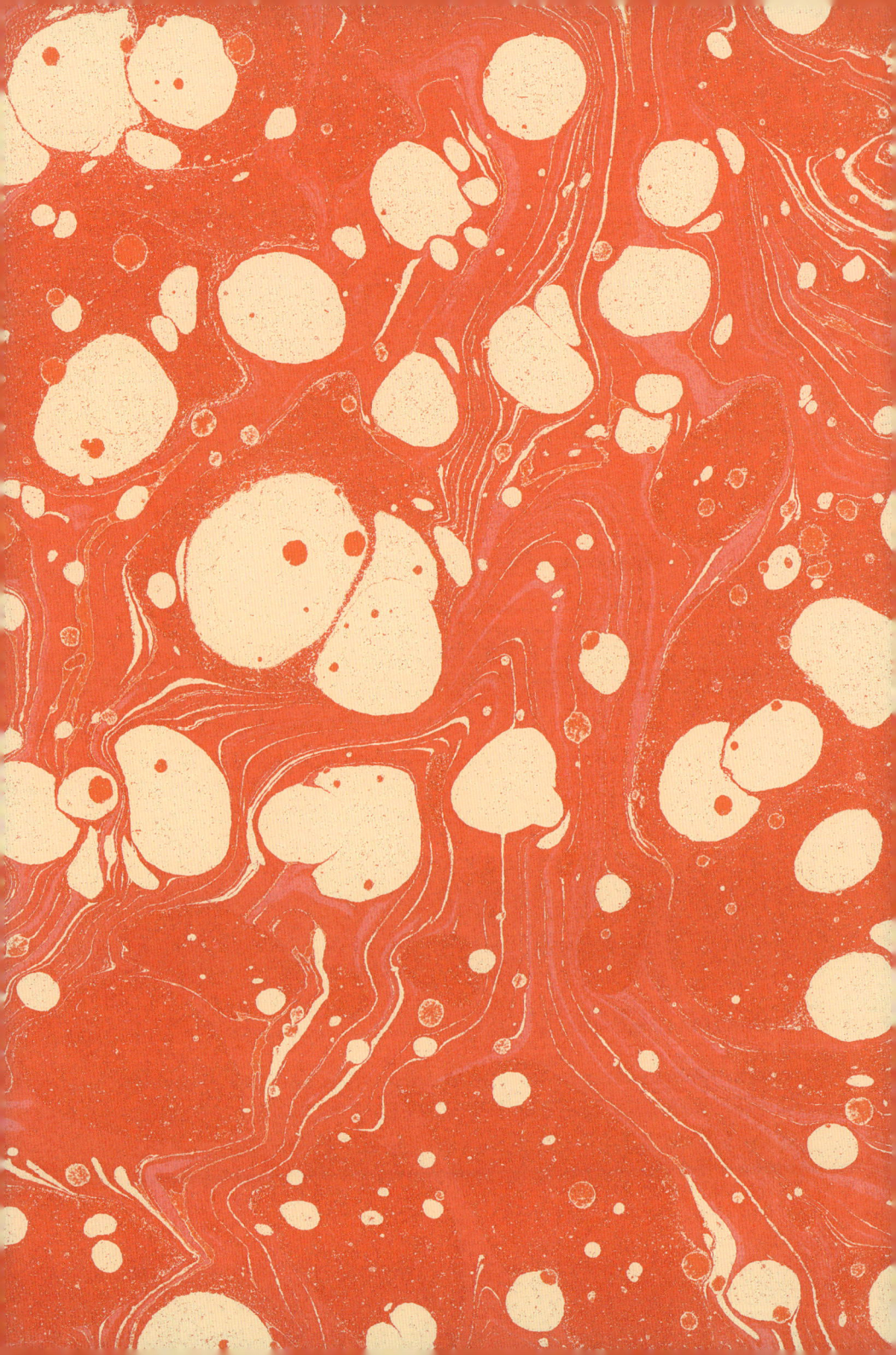

UNREQUITED

LOVE

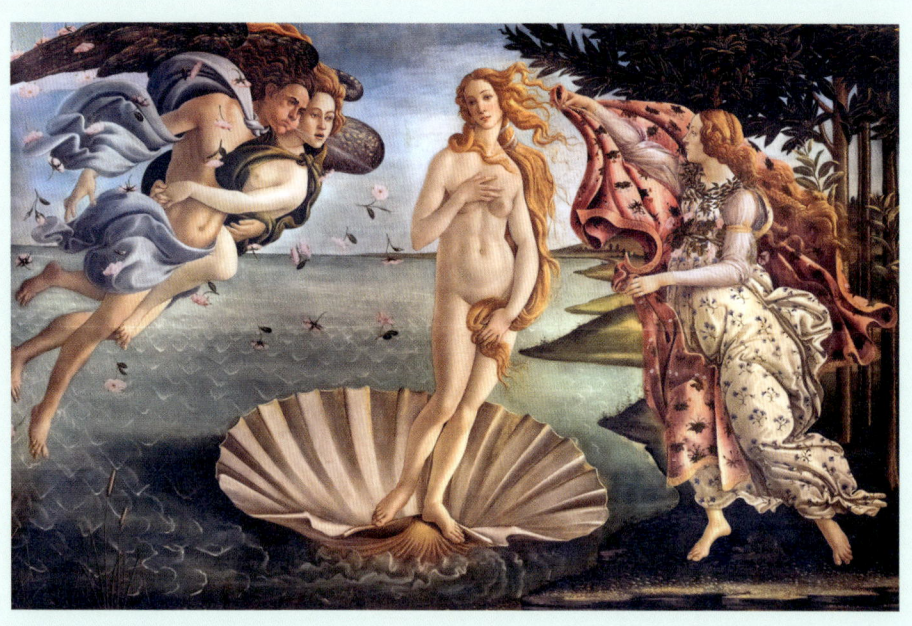

Birth of Venus, Sandro Botticelli, 1485

The Worship of Venus

Sandro Botticelli &
Simonetta Vespucci

O ne of the side effects of unrequited love is that the long-suffering, rejected lover often ends up idealizing the object of his or her obsession. They place them on a pedestal – beautiful, charismatic, endlessly desirable, yet remote and unobtainable. Is this the emotional truth behind the strange power of Sandro Botticelli's painting, the *Birth of Venus*? It has been so rumoured for centuries, but is there any substance to the idea?

Let's start with the facts. Made in 1485, when the Florentine artist was at the peak of his powers, this is one of the most revolutionary and compelling paintings in the history of Western art. It is the first erotic nude painted since antiquity; a life-sized depiction of Venus, the Roman goddess of love, who was born in adult form from the foam of the sea. Botticelli chooses the moment she is blown ashore by the wind gods Zephyr and Aura, riding on a giant scallop shell. The figure on the right, wearing a dress embroidered with flowers and welcoming Venus to the world is Hora – a goddess of spring.

But it is the naked Venus who is at the centre of the painting. She is a compelling figure, coy yet sensual, trying, but not quite succeeding, to cover her nudity with her arms and long flowing hair. The pose is not Botticelli's invention but one that derives originally from a sculpture known as the Cnidian Aphrodite, the equivalent of Venus, which was made by the great Greek sculptor, Praxiteles, in the 4th century BCE. It was copied many thousands of times by later Greek and Roman sculptors. Indeed, there was a version in the private collection of the Medicis – the rulers of Florence and Botticelli's most important patrons.

In classical art, Venus was always portrayed as the idealisation of beauty. But is this the case here? Or is she inspired by a real person – a woman who so obsessed or fascinated Botticelli that he cast her as a goddess? Rumours and legends abound about the connection between the painting and one particular woman whom Botticelli knew well – the most famous beauty of the age, Simonetta Vespucci. In fact, he not only knew her, he seems to have worshipped her. Just before he died in 1510 – many years after Simonetta's own demise – Botticelli asked to be buried in the same church, 'at her feet'.

But 'La Bella Simonetta' as she became known when she arrived in Florence from Genoa in 1469, was never, as far as we know, Botticelli's lover. Just 16 and recently married to an aristocrat called Marco Vespucci, she took Florentine society by storm. The Medicis, including Lorenzo, who was head of the family, were especially intrigued. In 1475, Lorenzo's younger brother Giuliano entered a splendid jousting tournament in the Piazza Santa Croce as Simonetta's champion. He carried her portrait painted on a huge (6ft x 3ft) banner.[70] It is now lost, but we know from a contemporary account that she was depicted as the goddess of wisdom, Pallas Athena, and the image was full of symbolism of her imperviousness to the temptations of love. Giuliano emerged victorious in the joust and declared Simonetta to be the tournament's 'Queen of Beauty'.

You might think that her husband, Marco, would feel a little insecure at this attention from such a powerful rival. Maybe he did. But it was also a normal part of an elaborate and important courtly tradition for a married woman to be

Is she inspired by a real person – a woman who so obsessed Botticelli that he cast her as a goddess?

championed by a young knight. As the imagery of the banner suggested, tradition dictated that his love must be spurned and the lady's virtue remain intact.

Most fascinating for us is that the banner was painted by Botticelli. So we know that ten years before the *Venus*, he had already painted Simonetta's portrait in the guise of a classical goddess. We can also assume that he knew her well for several years, because they both attended the same church and both were well-connected in the relatively small world of the Florentine court. But did he, like Giuliano, worship her from afar and was she the inspiration for the *Birth of Venus*?

No other portraits of Simonetta made in her lifetime now exist, so we can't be sure what she looked like. Some art historians have dismissed the idea that Simonetta was Botticelli's inspiration as 'romantic myth' and suggest we should see the *Venus* instead as an idealized representation of beauty, as many of the women in Botticelli's paintings seem to be. After all, she died, tragically young, in 1476, a decade before the painting was made.

But Botticelli, who never married,[71] was only 24 when Simonetta came to Florence. It is perfectly possible that his concept of an ideal beauty was inspired by her – in many ways it would be the obvious thing to do. There are also good reasons to connect Simonetta with the *Birth of Venus*. She herself was born in Porto Venere (Port of Venus) near Genoa. And, like the jousting banner, the painting was commissioned by one of the Medici family, most likely Giuliano's cousin, Lorenzo di Pierfrancesco.

What we certainly have to explain is why the painting – arguably Botticelli's greatest – has proved so powerful and enduring over so many centuries. Clearly, he was inspired, but was it by beauty or love? Perhaps it was by both, championed by a young knight. As the imagery of the banner suggested, tradition dictated that his love must be spurned and the lady's virtue remain intact.

The Nightmare, Henry Fuseli, 1781

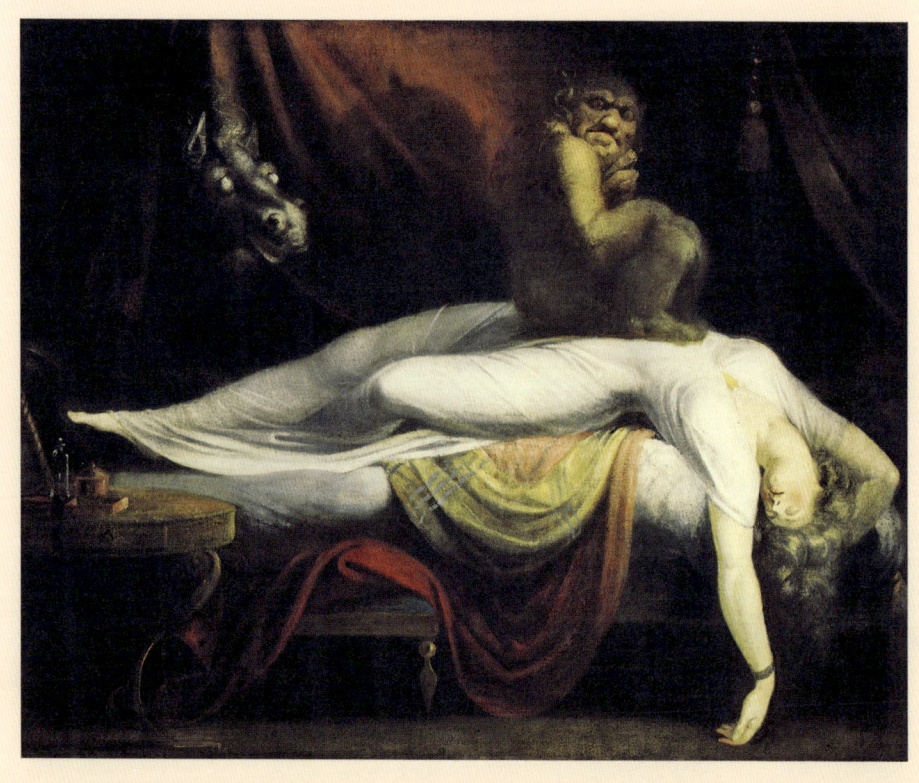

Stuff of Nightmares

Henry Fuseli & Anna Landolt

'Last night I had her in bed with me – tossed my bedclothes hugger-mugger – wound my hot and tight-clasped hands about her – fused her body and soul together with my own – poured into her my spirit, breath and strength. Anyone who touches her now commits adultery and incest! She is mine, and I am hers. And have her I will.' [72]

But have her he didn't. This letter was written – in defiance of reality – in 1779 by Henry Fuseli (1741–1825) to his friend Johann Kaspar Lavater after he had heard that the woman he loved was to marry another man. The woman, a young pianist called Anna Landolt, was Lavater's niece, whom Fuseli had recently met on a visit to Zurich (Fuseli was Swiss but had been living in London and Italy). As the letter suggests, he had fallen passionately – and possessively – in love with her. But his obsession had always been doomed. It is unclear whether Fuseli even felt able to confess his love directly to her. Either way, he missed his chance. Although he approached her father about the possibility of marriage, his suit was rejected – Fuseli was too poor to be a suitable husband.

However, the infatuation seems to have made a lasting impression on Fuseli's art. His most famous picture, *The Nightmare*, which he painted about 18 months later, is often seen as a reaction against – or even a revenge for – his rejection. The depiction of a sleeping or unconscious woman, oppressed by the goblin-like creature who sits on her stomach, while a traumatized horse with bulging eyes thrusts its head through the curtain behind is a deeply unsettling image. It shocked viewers when it was first exhibited in London in 1782 and still has a disturbing power today.

However, the implications of the image would have been understood rather differently when it was first made than they are today. The phrase 'night mare' referred not to the bad dream itself, but to the evil spirit which caused it. In the painting, Fuseli has conflated the mare (which was female) with an incubus, which was male, and another mythological creature driven by lust, who rode his horse through the night and preyed on sleeping women.

Given the frenzy of desire and fantasy expressed in Fuseli's letter to Lavater, it seems hard to believe that he didn't see some analogies between his own seething emotions and those of the incubus himself. He certainly made many explicit sketches of his highly charged, often fetishistic sexual fantasies. Lavater was later to describe Fuseli in terms that also echo the dark side of his passions. 'His spirits are hurricane, his servants flames of fire. He goes on the wings of the wind. His laugh is the mockery of Hell, and his love a murderous lightning flash.' [73]

The link between *The Nightmare* and Fuseli's unrequited feelings for Anna Landolt is made even more intriguing because of an unfinished portrait on the back of the same canvas. It depicts a refined and well-dressed woman with spectacular hair piled high on her head and a long tress cascading down her neck and over her shoulder. Her dark eyes stare intensely at the viewer and there seems to be a half smile on her face. Intriguingly, she seems to be holding a letter or a paper in her right hand, while with her left hand she toys with her hair. (Hair seems to have been a 'thing' for Fuseli and he used an image of a woman taunting a man with her long plait in one of his erotic sketches).

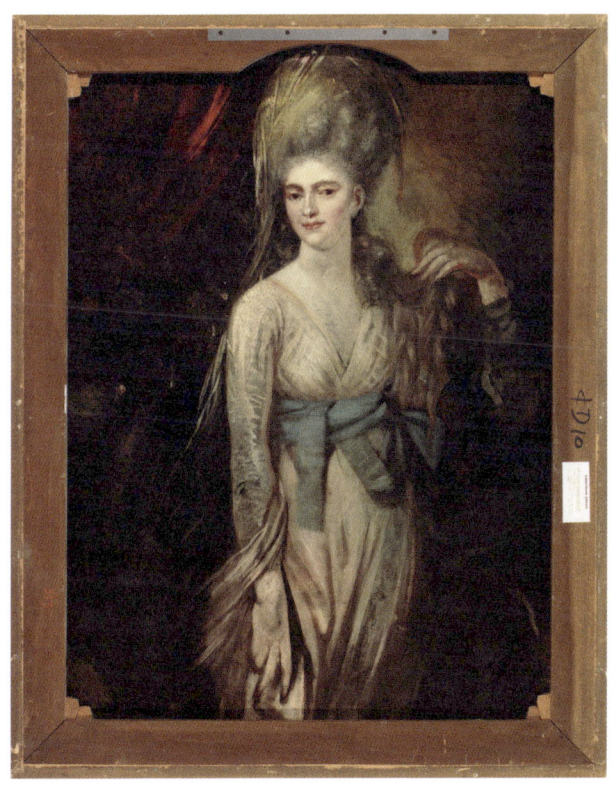

Portrait of a Lady, Henry Fuseli

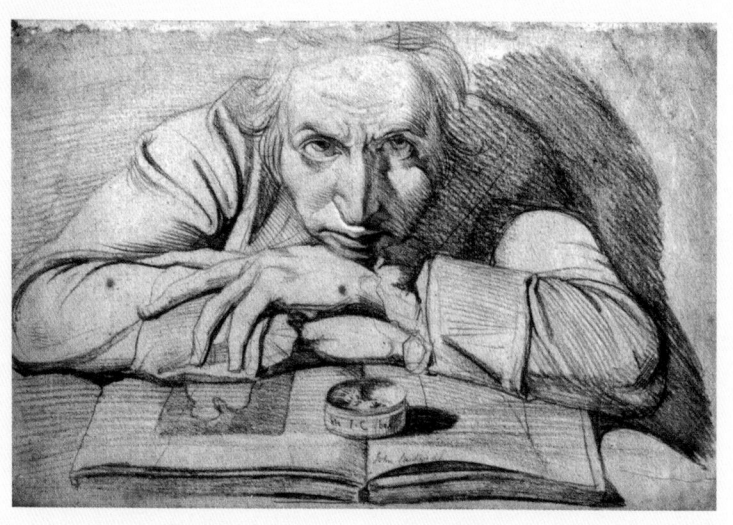

Self-Portrait, Henry Fuseli

She can't be identified for certain, but several scholars have suggested that it must represent Landolt and that she would have sat for Fuseli during his visit to Zurich. Is that where his passion was ignited? Is the letter significant? Did he confess his love to Anna?

We can't answer those questions for sure, but it does seem telling that Fuseli chose to re-use this canvas for *The Nightmare*. He could easily have overpainted the portrait, blocking it out with the new picture. But he chose instead to turn it around so that she would be forever linked to the vision of what amounts to a potential erotic assault – or certainly an incarnation of erotic dominance – on the reverse. Probably pushing things a little too far are a few critics who have found a resemblance between the portrait and the sleeping woman and even seen Fuseli's own face in that of the incubus.

It is, however, interesting to consider Fuseli's own idea of himself around this time. In a sketched self-portrait, his haunted, haggard face is hunched over an open book and a round box (inscribed with the initials of his friend, John Cartwright). With his doleful eyes staring up at the viewer, the defiance of his letter is an empty memory. He is every inch the rejected lover.

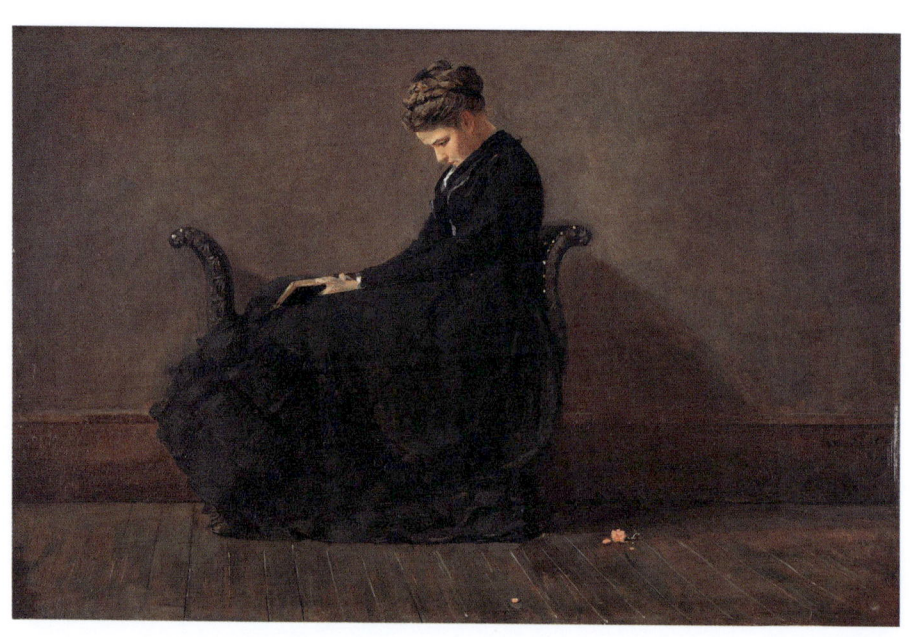

Portrait of Helena de Kay, Winslow Homer, 1871–1872

Like a Red, Red Rose

Winslow Homer & Helena de Kay

D ressed in black, eyes cast down, book closed symbolically in her lap: the figure in this portrait looks more like a woman in mourning than an object of love and adoration. The empty room, bare boards and colourless wall only add to a sense of emotional desolation. But, as we can see by the single red rose discarded on the floor, if this painting by Winslow Homer is about mourning, it is more concerned with lost love than with the death of an individual. A scattering of petals lies near the abandoned flower and we are left to guess at the narrative. Has it simply been rejected because it is past its prime? Has the woman plucked out the petals in a fret? Perhaps it was a love-offering which she has refused and it has been thrown down in frustration by another who has now left the room?

What we do know is that, for the sitter in this portrait, the artist Helena de Kay (1846–1916), a red rose was deeply meaningful. According to her best friend, Mary Hallock, it represented a sort of personal emblem, a symbol of herself.[74] We also know that the painting seems to be part of the process by which the artist, Winslow Homer (1836–1910), came to terms with his unrequited love for her.

The two had probably first met in the late 1860s in New York, when Homer was in his early 30s and developing a growing

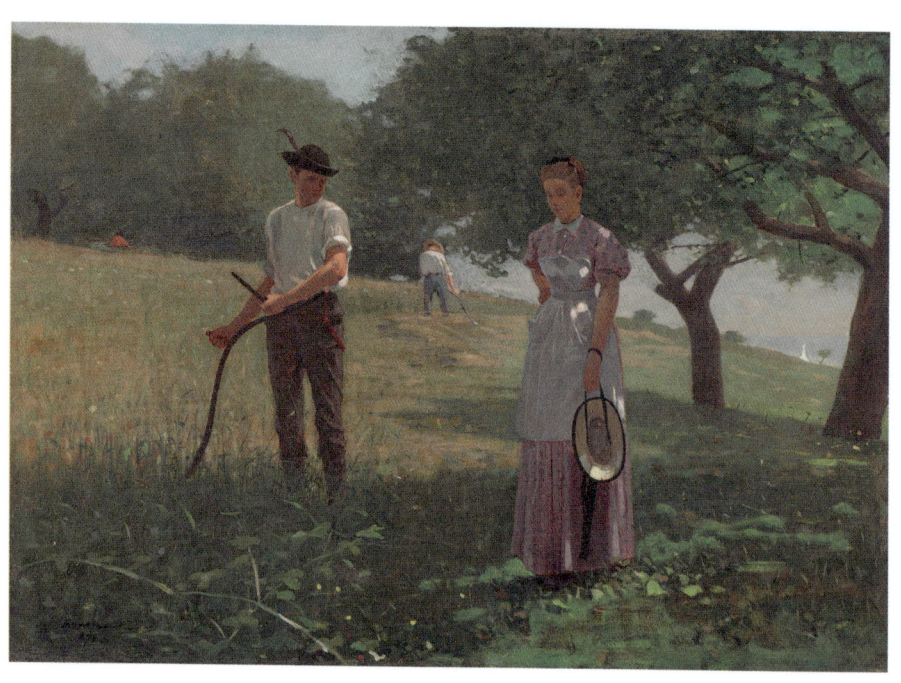

Waiting for an Answer, Winslow Homer, 1872

reputation as one of America's leading landscape and maritime artists and she was learning to paint watercolours. In the summer of 1872 they spent a significant amount of time in each other's company, probably in the Catskill Mountains where her family had a holiday home. During that time, Homer produced several paintings in which Helena acted as a model. In one, a butterfly seems about to alight on her hand. In another, she leans back against a hammock, deep in thought. They can barely be called portraits – her features are not quite clear enough to be seen in that way and there is a sense of distance and separateness to the compositions. It is as though she is like the fluttering butterfly, just beyond the reach of the artist. She is always in the shade, always preoccupied and she never catches the viewer's eye.

Most telling of all is *Waiting for an Answer* which is set in the same sun-drenched landscape. The title makes the narrative explicit, but we could probably guess the story in any case. A young man breaks from his work cutting long grass for the hay harvest. He holds his scythe in a moment of suspense – the woman to whom he has proposed has come to give him her answer. In the background, another worker continues to reap, while the suitor's world stands still as he awaits his fate.

We don't need to hear the answer to know what it is going to be. Theirs is not the shy body language of lovers drawn magnetically to each other. He is turning towards her, but she faces away. This is the moment of rejection. Their eyes are cast down; their faces are in shadow. She seems to have started speaking – a few words of comfort and kindness perhaps before she delivers her decision. His head has already begun to drop as his hope withers.

There is only one reason why Homer would choose to paint a scene such as this. Artists in love do not paint images of rejection when their heart is soaring with passion and expectation. He must also have sensed his own fate but, like the reaper, clings on to the last vestiges of optimism, even though his heart is sinking.

We don't know how realistic Homer felt his prospects might have been, as he was an intensely private man. The only evidence of his state of mind are the paintings he made and a handful of letters he sent to de Kay that year in which he at first yearns to see her, before the warmth drains out of the relationship. His chances had almost certainly never been good. Helena had already met the man who was to become her husband – the publisher Richard Watson Gilder. They married on 3 June 1874. Homer inscribed the same date on the bottom right corner of his portrait of Helena dressed in black and gave it to her as a wedding gift. It is hardly the most cheering of images to mark such an occasion, but perhaps his intentions were a sincere reminder of the depth of his feelings for her. After all, the painting was almost certainly made in 1872 when – after that golden summer – he realized his love for her was doomed. It was a disappointment from which he never seems to have recovered. Homer lived alone for the rest of his life.

After that golden summer, he realized his love for her was doomed.

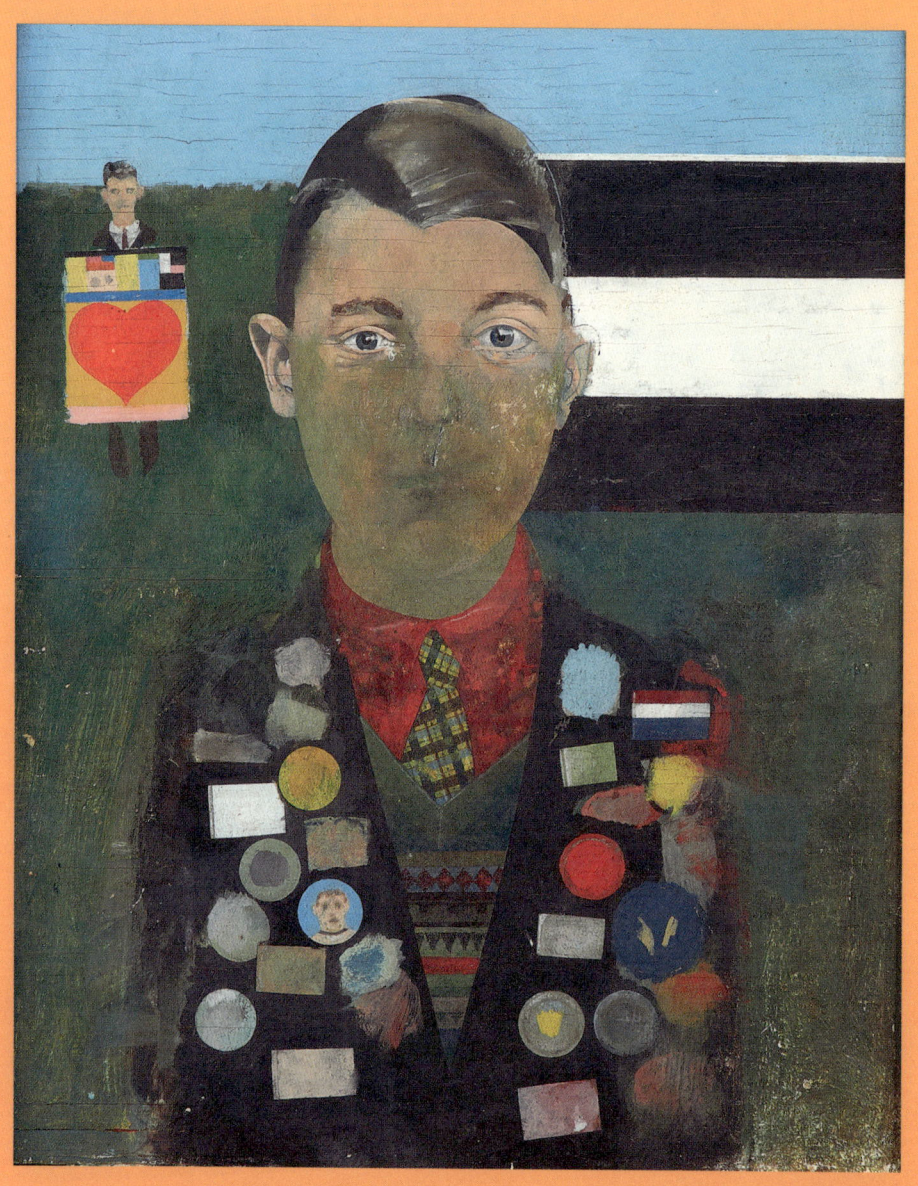

Boy With Paintings, Peter Blake, 1957–1959

Valentine's Verdict

Peter Blake & Pauline Boty

There is a story behind *Boy With Paintings*, both visually and in real life. It was made by the pop artist, Peter Blake (b.1932), between 1957–1959 as a double self-portrait. In the background, an apparently younger version of himself – wearing a black suit and tie and a white shirt – holds up a brightly coloured painting dominated by a red heart. It's an image of the over-sized Valentine's Day card that Blake himself had recently given to the artist Pauline Boty (1938–1966).

Another self-portrait dominates the foreground. The lower part of his face has taken on green smudges from the surrounding colour field, but his eyes are crystal clear and forming in the corner of one of them is a large tear. The Valentine's Day card has been rejected. He remains alone, his love unrequited. The image isn't entirely bleak. His black jacket has blossomed with colourful badges and his plain white shirt has been replaced with a bright red one, a tartan tie and a vibrant jumper. But the overall sense is of melancholy and rejection. Indeed, Blake seems to be conjuring up echoes of another lonely figure – the sad clown, Pierrot, who is depicted with arms down by his sides gazing sadly at us out of a famous painting by Antoine Watteau (1684–1721). In Italian comic tradition, Pierrot is abandoned by his lover Columbine (see p98).

Boty, the object of Blake's unrequited love, was then a 20-year-old student at the Royal College of Art. She was astonishingly beautiful. Dubbed 'the Wimbledon Bardot' by her school friends because of her resemblance to the French film star, she was offered modelling and acting roles (she made a brief appearance with Michael Caine in *Alfie*). However, her first passion was art and she was soon to become – along with Blake – one of the leading figures of the British pop art scene.

Her romantic rejection did not undermine their friendship, nor their artistic relationship. Indeed, Boty's first major exhibition was held jointly with Blake and two other artists: *Pauline Boty, Peter Blake, Christine Porter, Geoffrey Reeve* at the AIA Gallery in London in late 1961. And, in 1962, a landmark BBC Monitor documentary, *Pop Goes the Easel*, made by the young Ken Russell, featured Blake and Boty together with Peter Phillips and Derek Boshier. (It also includes a very brief appearance of a dancing David Hockney.) In a fascinating insight into London life just before the Swinging Sixties, the artists were profiled as representatives of a new type of art which took its inspiration from, and reflected on, popular rather than high culture. It includes a slightly self-conscious moment when Blake and Boty discuss some of her collages.

A year later, both were married to other people: Blake to the artist Jann Haworth[75] and, only ten days after meeting him, Boty to the literary agent, Clive Goodwin (1932–1978) – 'the very first man I met who really liked women ... the first man I could talk very freely to'.[76]

It seems that Boty may also have been on the rebound. That same year – perhaps before meeting Goodwin in the summer or perhaps soon after – she made one of her best-known works. In an apparent homage to Blake, *My Colouring Book* also used Valentine imagery and the hearts are similar in shape to that on his card to her. This time though, the giant double hearts at the centre of the painting are in doleful shades of blue. Boty adapted a series of rhyming couplets derived from the lyrics of a

Pauline Boty, 1963

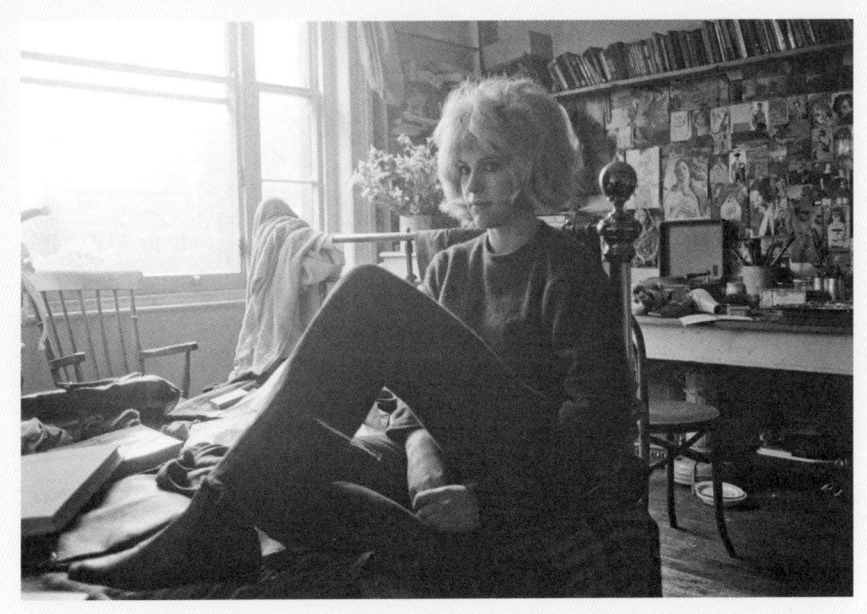

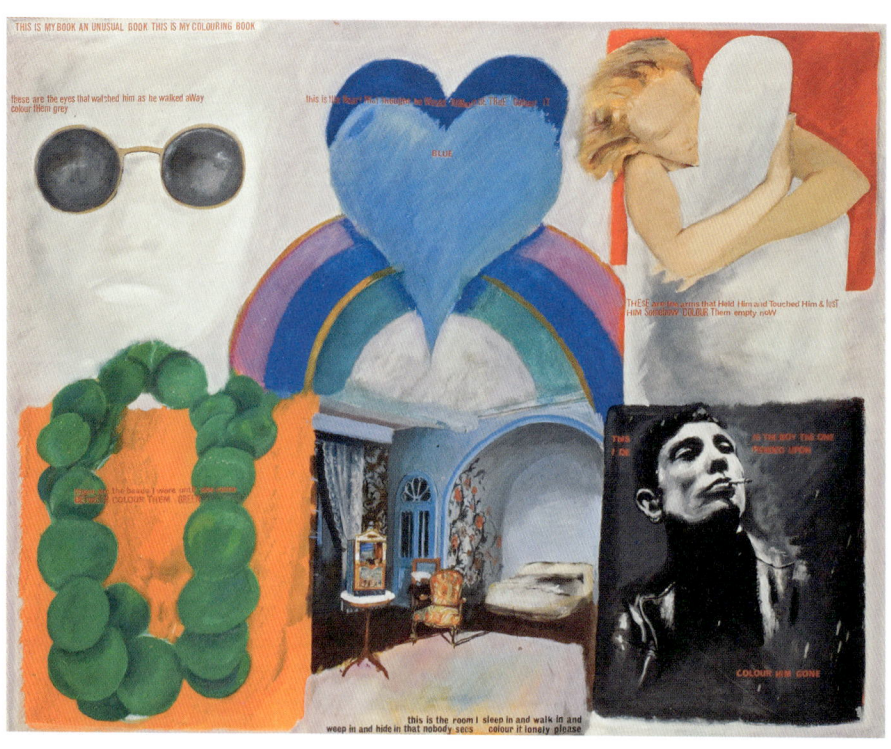

My Colouring Book, Pauline Boty, 1963

pop song of the same name which had hit the charts in 1962.[77]
She uses them as captions for six overlapping scenes laid out like
episodes in a comic book and depicted in a rainbow of colours.
The final scene, however, is in black and white – a depiction of
an aloof male figure in a leather jacket. Boty captions it with an
adaptation of the last line of the song, which is broken up by the
figure of the man and written out in capital letters.

THIS   IS THE BOY THE ONE
I DE   PENDED UPON

COLOUR HIM GONE

The original line read: 'This is the man whose love I
depended upon/Colour him gone'. She has emasculated her
former lover (who was never identified and may have been
generic), removed the word love and drained all colour from
the image.

Only three years later, Boty's life was to be cut tragically
short. In June 1965, when pregnant with her daughter Katy, she
was diagnosed with cancer. She refused to have an abortion or to
receive chemotherapy which might have damaged the baby. Katy
was born in February 1966. Pauline died on 1 July, aged 28.

Half a century later, in 2018, Blake (by now Sir Peter)
memorialized her in his print, *BBC2 Remembering Pauline Boty,*
a photographic collage of presenters, characters and comedians
from five decades of BBC programmes gathered in front of the
former Television Centre building in Shepherd's Bush. It's like
a rush of sentimental visual memories and Boty is the most
prominent of them all. She stands in the foreground, cigarette
in hand, as though she is the master of ceremonies.

Acknowledgements

*I'm indebted to the insights of many experts and curators
I have talked to in recent years, especially those at The
Courtauld Institute, The National Gallery, Tate, the Royal
Academy of Arts and the University of East Anglia. Special
thanks are also due to: Sandy Heslop, Tracy Jones, Laura
Paton, Philippa Sitters, Emily Taylor, Dan Jackson, Sarah
Cook, Louise Frith, Chris Gatcum and Carron Brown.*

Notes

[1] Katlijne van der Stighelen, Geert van der Snickt, Gerlinde Gruber and Koen Janssens, 'Helena Fourment further uncovered. A new interpretation of "Het Pelsken" based on recent analytical imaging' in Rubens in Private: The Master Portrays His Family by Ben van Beneden (editor). London: Thames and Hudson, 2015.

[2] It was presented to the Hispanic Society of America in 1907.

[3] Sarah Greenough (editor), My Faraway One: Selected Letters of Georgia O'Keeffe and Alfred Stieglitz, Volume 1 1915–1933. New Haven: Yale University Press, 2011, p150.

[4] https://www.metmuseum.org/art/collection/search/817970 (Accessed on 21 March 2024.)

[5] https://www.metmuseum.org/art/collection/search/271570 (Accessed on 11 March 2024.)

[6] Sarah Greenough (editor), My Faraway One: Selected Letters of Georgia O'Keeffe and Alfred Stieglitz, Volume 1 1915–1933. New Haven: Yale University Press, 2011, p298.

[7] https://www.artic.edu/articles/838/okeeffes-shells-and-bones (Accessed on 11 March 2024.)

[8] Anna C. Chave, 'O'Keeffe and the Masculine Gaze', Art in America, Vol 78, Jan 1990, pp114–179.

[9] https://www.brooklynmuseum.org/eascfa/about/feminist_art_base/sylvia-sleigh (Accessed on 11 March 2024.)

[10] https://www.brooklynmuseum.org/eascfa/about/feminist_art_base/sylvia-sleigh (Accessed on 11 March 2024.)

[11] H. Perry Chapman, Wouter Th. Kloek and Arthur K. Wheelock Jr, Jan Steen: Painter and Storyteller. New Haven: Yale University Press, 1996, p126.

[12] H. Perry Chapman, Wouter Th. Kloek and Arthur K. Wheelock Jr, Jan Steen: Painter and Storyteller. New Haven: Yale University Press, 1996, p12.

[13] Quoted in Jackie Wullschläger, Chagall: A Biography. New York: Knopf, 2008, p89.

[14] Bella Chagall, First Encounter. New York: Schocken Books, 1983, p197.

[15] Jackie Wullschläger, Chagall: A Biography. New York: Knopf, 2008, pp375–376.

[16] The inscription continues: 'I painted these pictures in the delightful city of San Francisco California for our companion Mr. Albert Bender, and it was in the month of April of the year 1931.' The original reads: 'Aquí nos veis, a mí, Frida Kahlo, junto con mi amado esposo Diego Rivera. Pinté estos retratos en la bella ciudad de San Francisco, California, para nuestro amigo Mr. Albert Bender y fue en el mes de abril del año 1931.'

[17] https://www.artgallery.nsw.gov.au/artboards/frida-kahlo-diego-rivera/mexicanidad/item/801bdg (Accessed on 11 March 2024.)

[18] Diego Rivera, 'Frida Kahlo y el arte mexicano' in Boletín del Seminario de Cultura Mexicana, No 2, Mexico DF, Oct 1943. Also quoted (in Spanish) at https://www.denverartmuseum.org/en/blog/quotes-diego-rivera. (Accessed on 11 March 2024). The translation is the author's.

[19] Giorgio Vasari (author), George Bull (translator), Lives of the Artists, Volume One. London: Penguin Classics, 2003, p216.

[20] Jeffrey Ruda, Fra Filippo Lippi: Life and Work – with a Complete Catalogue. London: Phaidon, 1993, plate 328.

[21] David Ekserdjian and Tom Henry, Raphael. London: National Gallery, 2022, pp286–287.

[22] Giorgio Vasari (author), Julia Conaway Bondanella and Peter Bondanella (trans), The Lives of the Artists. Oxford: OUP, 1991, p336.

[23] Giorgio Vasari (author), Gaston du C. de Vere (translator), The Lives of the Painters, Sculptors and Architects. London: Everyman's Library, 1996, p732.

[24] Some art historians reject the idea that this is a portrait, arguing that it instead represents an 'ideal of beauty'. But that doesn't seem to square with the highly specific treatment of the sitter's left breast, which seems to be slightly deformed. Some analyses have even suggested that she may be suffering from a tumour in her breast and point to what seems to be a slight swelling in the gland of her armpit, which would be consistent with such a condition.

[25] Femme demi-nue couchée: la rose

[26] Douglas Cooper, 'Renoir, Lise and the Le Cœur Family: A Study of Renoir's Early Development - 1 Lise' in The Burlington Magazine, Vol 101, No 674, May 1959, pp. 162–171. Also see: John Collins, 'Tréhot, Lise' in Dictionary of Artists' Models by Jill Berk Jiminez (editor). New York: Routledge, 2001, p526 (and the following pages).

[27] Kristin Schroeder, 'A New Objectivity: Fashionable Surfaces in Lotte Laserstein's New Woman Pictures' in The Art Bulletin, Vol 101, No 4, Dec 2019, pp95–116.

[28] Caroline Stroude and Adrian Stroude, 'Lotte Laserstein and the German Naturalist Tradition' in the Woman's Art Journal, Vol 9, No 1 (Spring – Summer, 1988), pp35–38.

[29] Carina Rech 'Intimate Distance: Queering the Art of Lotte Laserstein' in Lotte Laserstein: A Divided Life by Anna-Carola Krausse (editor) and Iris Müller-Westermann (editor). Munich: Hirmer, 2024, p98.

[30] Reproduced here: https://guide.modernamuseet.se/stockholm/en/collection/lotte-laserstein/jag-och-min-modell/

[31] https://collections.artsmia.org/art/142336/sarah-bernhardt-with-a-cat-georges-antoine-rochegrosse (Accessed on 5 March 2024.)

[32] Picasso: The Beauty and the Beast, first broadcast on BBC2, 2023.

[33] John Richardson, A Life of Picasso, Vol III: The Triumphant Years, 1917–1932. London: Jonathan Cape, 2007, p323.

[34] Lytton Strachey to Carrington, 11 July 1919, quoted in A Life of Dora Carrington 1893–1932 by Gretchen Gerzina. London: Pimlico, 1995, p148.

[35] Virginia Woolf to Vanessa Bell, 17 January 1918, quoted in The Question of Things Happening – The Letters of Virginia Woolf 1912–1922 by Virginia Woolf (author), Nigel Nicolson (editor) and Joanne Trautmann (assistant editor). London: Hogarth, 1976, p211.

[36] Carrington to Lytton Strachey, 14 May 1921, quoted in Carrington's Letters by Anne Chisholm (editor). London: Chatto & Windus, 2017, p170.

[37] Carrington to Brenan, 30 August 1921, quoted in Carrington's Letters by Anne Chisholm (editor). London: Chatto & Windus, 2017, p184.

[38] Carrington to Alix Strachey, no date, Lytton Strachey Trust, quoted in A Life of Dora Carrington 1893–1932 by Gretchen Gerzina. London: Pimlico, 1995, p210.

[39] Carrington to Brenan, 21 July 1925 (University of Texas at Austin), quoted in A Life of Dora Carrington 1893–1932 by Gretchen Gerzina. London: Pimlico, 1995, pp228-229.

[40] Michael Holroyd, Lytton Strachey: The New Biography. London: Vintage, 1995, p678.

[41] Dora Carrington (author) and David Garnett (editor), Carrington: Letters and Extracts from her Diaries. London: Jonathan Cape, 1970, p495.

42 https://www.theguardian.com/
artanddesign/2021/oct/27/two-lovers-kiss-
behind-a-tree-clifford-prince-kings-best-
photograph (Accessed on 12 March 2024.)

43 https://planetwoo.itv.com/posts/clifford-
prince-king-love-songs-interview (Accessed
on 12 March 2024.)

44 https://planetwoo.itv.com/posts/clifford-
prince-king-love-songs-interview (Accessed
on 12 March 2024.)

45 https://www.theguardian.com/
artanddesign/2021/oct/27/two-lovers-kiss-
behind-a-tree-clifford-prince-kings-best-
photograph (Accessed on 12 March 2024.)

46 https://planetwoo.itv.com/posts/clifford-
prince-king-love-songs-interview (Accessed
on 12 March 2024.)

47 https://planetwoo.itv.com/posts/clifford-
prince-king-love-songs-interview (Accessed
on 12 March 2024.)

48 https://planetwoo.itv.com/posts/clifford-
prince-king-love-songs-interview (Accessed
on 12 March 2024.)

49 https://mydailyartdisplay.uk/2013/09/06/
suzanne-valadon-part-7-the-final-years/
(Accessed on 12 March 2024.)

50 Catherine Hewitt, Renoir's Dancer: The
Secret Life of Suzanne Valadon. London: Icon
Books, 2017, p215.

51 Cahiers d'Art, 10: 5–6, October 1935,
127 in Man Ray / Lee Miller: Partners in
Surrealism by Phillip Prodger (translator).
London: Merrell Publishers, 2011, p45.

52 Man Ray, Self-Portrait. London: Penguin
Books, 1963, p255.

53 Carolyn Burke, Lee Miller: A Life. New
York: Knopf, 2005, p89.

54 Carolyn Burke, Lee Miller: A Life. New
York: Knopf, 2005, p89.

55 Baroness Kizette de Lempicka-Foxhall
and Charles Phillips, Passion by Design: The
Art and Times of Tamara de Lempicka. New
York: Abbeville Press Publishers, second
edition, 2000, pp90–91.

56 Baroness Kizette de Lempicka-Foxhall
and Charles Phillips, Passion by Design:
The Art and Times of Tamara de Lempicka.
New York: Abbeville Press Publishers,
second edition, 2000, pp90–91.

57 John Gruen, The Artist Observed:
28 Interviews with Contemporary
Artists. Atlanta: A Cappella Books, 1991, p3.

58 https://www.theguardian.com/
artanddesign/2017/feb/24/francis-bacons-
first-portrait-of-lover-george-dyer-to-go-on-
sale-1964-triptych-roald-dahl (Accessed on
12 March 2024.)

59 Interview with Francis Giacobetti.
Extract published in The Art Newspaper,
1 June 2003. https://www.theartnewspaper.
com/2003/06/01/francis-giacobetti-
interviews-francis-bacon-i-painted-to-be-
loved (Accessed on 12 March 2024.)

60 Norman Bryson et al., Francis Bacon and
the Tradition of Art. Milan: Skira, 2004,
p360.

61 Sue Roe, The Private Lives of the
Impressionists. New York: Harper Collins,
2006, p103.

62 No clear blood-line has yet been proved
and it seems more likely to be a family
myth than a reality. See: Clairre Gooden,
Fragonard and Morisot: Resolving the Family
Connection, in Marriane Mathieu (ed),
Berthe Morisot, Shaping Impressionism.
London: Dulwich Picture Gallery, 2023,
pp.78–89; Sylvie Patry, Berthe Morisot:
Woman Impressionist. New York: Rizzoli,
2018, pp. 93–97; and Jean-Dominique Rey,
Berthe Morisot. Paris: Flammarion, 2023,
p50.

63 There are 11 oil paintings; he also made
other sketches and drawings.

[64] Otto Dix to Hans Kinkel, 1948, quoted in Dix in Düsseldorf (ex. cat.) by Galerie Remmert und Barth. Düsseldorf 2011, p120.

[65] Karin Schick, Otto Dix, Hommage à Martha. Berlin: Hatje Cantz, 2005, pp64–69.

[66] Harry Mathews' contributions to: Niki de Saint Phalle, Harry and Me, 1950–1960: The Family Years. Salenstein: Benteli, 2006, p120.

[67] https://www.tate.org.uk/art/artworks/saint-phalle-shooting-picture-t03824 (Accessed on 12 March 2024.)

[68] https://www.christies.com/en/lot/lot-4740059 (Accessed on 12 March 2024.)

[69] https://www.moma.org/artists/1444 (Accessed on 12 March 2024.)

[70] For a detailed account of the joust and the banner, see R.W. Lightbown, Sandro Botticelli: Life and Work. London: Thames and Hudson, 1989, pp61–65.

[71] In 1502, Botticelli was accused of sodomy with one of his assistants. It was a common way to attempt to damage a rival and he was never charged. (See R.W. Lightbown, Sandro Botticelli: Life and Work. London: Thames and Hudson, 1989, p302.)

[72] Letter to Johann Kaspar Lavater, 16 June 1779, quoted in Fuseli: The Nightmare by Nicholas Powell. London: Allen Lane, 1973, p60.

[73] Eudo C. Mason, The Mind of Henry Fuseli, London: Routledge & Kegan Paul Limited, 1951, p67.

[74] Hallock wrote that when she married, de Kay 'sent me the red rose we called hers, her type and symbol, to wear inside my wedding dress – I have it still, a few petals empurpled with age, pressed inside an old locket.' From Rodman W. Paul (editor), A Victorian Gentlewoman in the Far West: The Reminiscences of Mary Hallock Foote. San Marino: The Huntington Library, 1972, p105.

[75] They divorced in 1979 and Blake married his current wife, Chrissy Wilson, in 1987.

[76] Nell Dunn, Talking to Women, London: Macgibbon and Kee, 1965, p23.

[77] 'My Coloring Book', by Fred Ebb and John Kander. First performed by Sandy Stewart.

Index

Picture Credits

Front cover, 61 Art: © Banco de México Diego Rivera Frida Kahlo Museums Trust, Mexico, D.F./DACS 2024. Photo: © Fine Art Images/ Bridgeman Images **Endpapers, 8, 12, 44, 64, 96, 122, 148, 168** Getty Images **14** Gift of Mr. and Mrs. Charles Wrightsman, in honour of Sir John Pope-Hennessy, 1981/The Metropolitan Museum of Art **17** Magite Historic/Alamy Stock Photo **20** GL Archive/Alamy Stock Photo **23** incamerastock / Alamy Stock Photo **24** Album/Alamy Stock Photo **26** SJArt/Alamy Stock Photo **28** Photo: Christian Franzen y Nissen © Museo Sorolla, Madrid **31** Iberfoto/Bridgeman Images **32** Cultural Archive/Alamy Stock Photo **35** Cultural Archive/Alamy Stock Photo **36** Art: © Georgia O'Keeffe Museum/DACS 2024. Photo: Museum of Fine Arts, Houston/Museum, purchase funded by the Agnes Cullen Arnold Endowment Fund/Bridgeman Images **38** Object: The David and Alfred Smart Museum of Art, The University of Chicago; Purchase, Paul and Miriam Kirkley Fund for Acquisitions. Image: Photograph © 2024 courtesy of The David and Alfred Smart Museum of Art, The University of Chicago **41** Dennis Hallinan/Alamy Stock Photo **46** Mauritshuis, Netherlands – Public Domain https://www. europeana.eu/item/2021672/resource_document_mauritshuis_818 **49** Artefact/Alamy Stock Photo **50** incamerastock/Alamy Stock Photo **52** Art: © ADAGP, Paris and DACS, London 2024. Photo: Bridgeman Images **57** Art: © ADAGP, Paris and DACS, London 2024. Photo: © Photo Scala, Florence **58** Art: © Banco de México Diego Rivera Frida Kahlo Museums Trust, Mexico, D.F./DACS 2024. Photo: © San Francisco Museum of Modern Art/Bridgeman Images **62** Art: © Banco de México Diego Rivera Frida Kahlo Museums Trust, Mexico, D.F./DACS 2024. Photo: © Mus. Associates/LACMA/Art Resource/ Scala **69** incamerastock/Alamy Stock Photo **70** Photo Scala, Florence **72** Carlo Bollo/Alamy Stock Photo **74** Keith Corrigan/Alamy Stock Photo **77** Artefact/Alamy Stock Photo **78** Bridgeman Images **82** Shim Harno/Alamy Stock Photo **84 (top)** Heritage Image Partnership Ltd/Alamy Stock Photo **84 (bottom)** Chester Dale Collection **86** incamerastock/Alamy Stock Photo **89** Album/Alamy Stock Photo **90** Art: © DACS 2024. Photo: Lotte Laserstein Archiv Krausse, Berlin **94** Art: © DACS 2024. Photo: Galerie Bassenge **98** Artepics/Alamy Stock Photo **101** © Daniel Katz Gallery **102 (top)** Photo © RMN-Grand Palais/Mathieu Rabeau/Scala Archives **102 (bottom)** © Coll. Comédie-Française **104** Art: © Succession Picasso/DACS, London

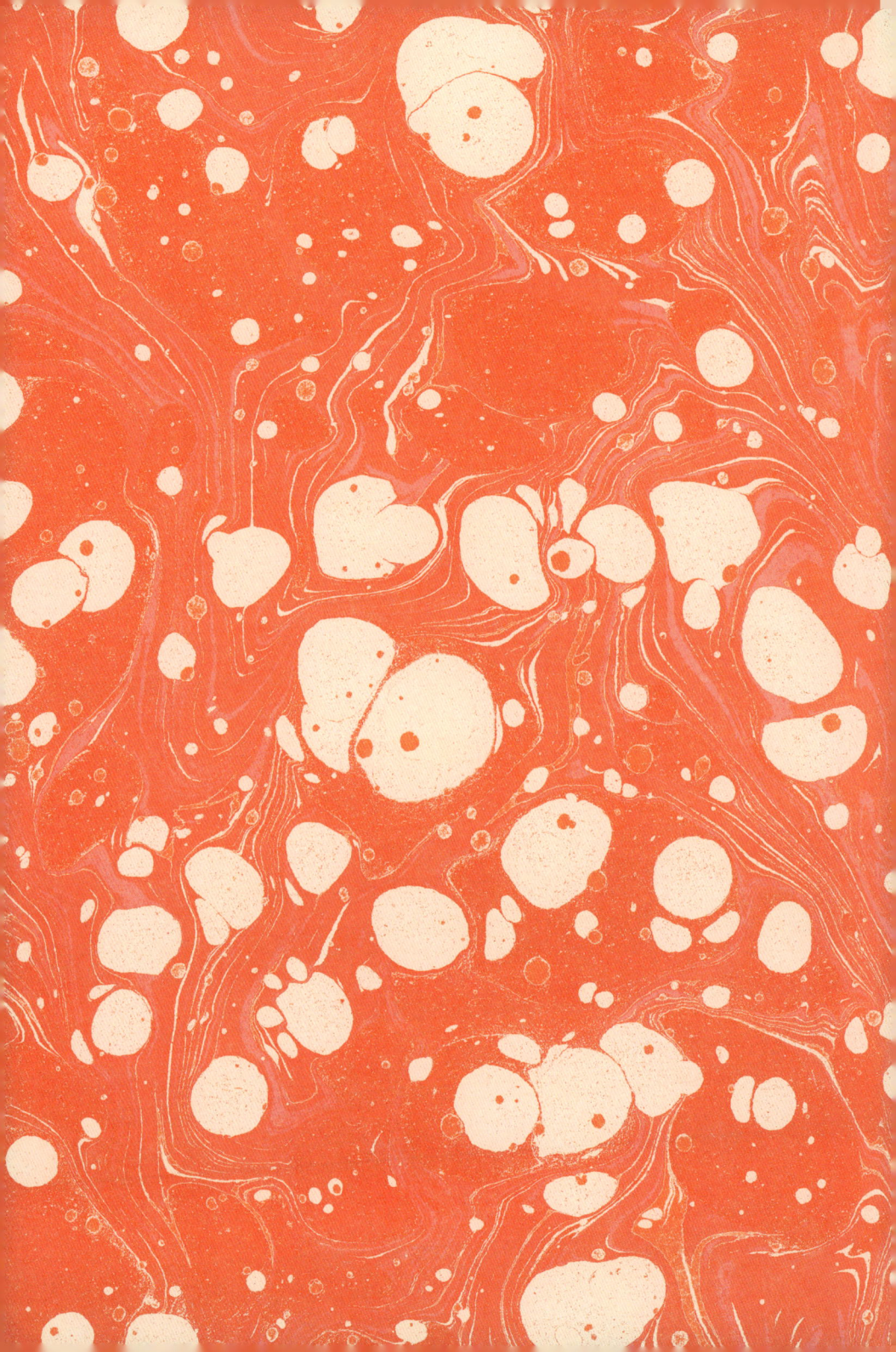